yland

FRONTIERLAND

TOMORROWLAND

50 Years
of Happiness

Disneyland

Then, Now, and Forever

by Bruce Gordon & Tim O'Day

DISNEY
EDITIONS
NEW YORK

Disneyland: Then, Now, and Forever Copyright © 2005 Disney Enterprises, Inc.

EDITIONS
NEW YORK

Written by Bruce Gordon & Tim O'Day

Printed in Singapore.

For information address Disney Editions, 114 Fifth Avenue, New York, New York 10011–5690.

We would like to sincerely thank and acknowledge the following individuals for their considerable contributions of support, encouragement, knowledge and expertise to the creation of this book: Marty Sklar, Michael Mendenhall, Duncan Wardle, Jay Rasulo, Michael Eisner, Jody Revenson, and Wendy Lefkon. Jess Allen, Julie Andrews, Tony Baxter, Suzanne Bonfiglio, Todd Bruechert, Denise Brown, Roberta Brubaker, Annika Chase, Hugh Chitwood, Tim Choy, Rebecca Cline, Jim Cora, Guy Cunningham, Alice Davis, Ron Dominguez, Greg Emmer, Howard Green, Pat Harris, John Hench, Paul Hiffmeyer, Jason Hoffman, Mike Jusko, TC Knoch, Jeff Kurtti, Jack Lindquist, Leonard Maltin, Page Martin, John McClintock, Gary Miereanu, Cathy Moorefield, David Mumford, Ed Nowak, Cicely Rigdon, George Savvas, Steve Sauer, Tracy Schlaepfer, Richard Sherman, Diane Scoglio, Betsy Singer, John Singh, Ed Squair, Dave Smith, Dave Stern, Robert Tieman, Melora Watson, Bryan Wittman, Dan Wolf.

For Disney Editions
Editorial Director: Wendy Lefkon
Editor: Jody Revenson

A Camphor Tree Book
Design by Bruce Gordon

Library of Congress Cataloging-in-Publication Data on file.
ISBN: 0-7868-5446-4
First Edition

Introduction

One memory I'll cherish forever is the thrill of seeing Disneyland for the first time. And guess who my tour guide was? Walt Disney! People just stopped and stared at him, they couldn't believe it was him. They recognized him, they reached out their hands to touch him—they were absolutely beaming and so was he—and so was I.

I have been to Disneyland many times since with my children, and now my grandchildren, but nothing will top that moment. It seemed you could see the whole park reflected in his eyes, his dream had come true. A dream that we could all share—and we did, we do, and we shall as long as there is a child left in each of us.

Disneyland was Walt's gift to a weary world. Once you pass through its gates the stress and strife of our everyday reality seems to melt away, and we enter a truly timeless realm that has withstood trends and fads to become a national treasure. Most importantly though, over the past fifty years more than six generations of family and friends from all over the world have gathered together in this happy place to experience its special brand of magic and the gifts of laughter, fun, nostalgia, fantasy, and adventure.

When Walt declared on Opening Day that "Disneyland is your land," I'm not sure if he truly realized how people everywhere would embrace the park as their own. No other form of entertainment is as universally beloved and cherished as Disneyland by people of all ages, backgrounds, and origins.

As people come to Disneyland during its "Happiest Homecoming on Earth" celebration to mark its 50th anniversary they will experience a park that is as vibrant and relevant today as it was in 1955. Disneyland is fifty years young and yet ageless.

As you read through this book I hope that it will rekindle fond memories for you, as it did for me. The following pages are a testament to the ideal that as the world changes and becomes more and more frenetic, we can always be assured that Disneyland will always be with us—then, now, and forever.

Julie Andrews

Honorary Homecoming Ambassador
Disneyland 50th Anniversary Celebration

HOMECOMING

ABOVE: *Sleeping Beauty Castle, awash with gold for the 50th Anniversary celebration.*

The Happiest Homecoming On Earth

Once upon a time, a dreamer named Walt Disney went looking for a special place where he could enjoy memorable moments with his two daughters. It was 1955 and the world was changing—changing from the fear of the "atomic age" to the frenzy of the "space age." In this era of uncertain transition Walt was looking for a magical place where, as he said, "parents and children could have fun together."

Discouraged by what he found, Walt summoned all of his considerable creative powers and an array of talented artisans to create what would become the single greatest entertainment achievement of the twentieth century—a place called Disneyland—a magical kingdom everyone could call their own. In creating Disneyland, Walt Disney sparked the world's imagination and established a beloved home for the young-at-heart of all ages.

The heartbeat of this home is to be found in the more than six generations of families and friends from across America and around the world who have grown up with the familiar and comforting experience of Disneyland, making it a treasured part of our collective consciousness. The Park is also unique due to the heartfelt affection people everywhere feel for their Disneyland.

Through the years, Disneyland has become a consistent source of joy and inspiration for the more than 500 million guests who have called it theirs, and the fulfillment of a dream for those who yearned to experience it for the first time. And, unlike many other passages of life that can't be repeated, you can always come back home to Disneyland.

Walt's dream lives on as the original Magic Kingdom celebrates its 50th Anniversary, and guests become active participants in a most extraordinary Homecoming, where every day is a golden celebration and every night is a glittering party. And not unlike a joyous family reunion or an endearing visit home, everyone is sure to leave Disneyland with the most treasured souvenir of all—incredible memories of a most remarkable event, thus ensuring that Disneyland will remain in their hearts for generations to come.

Chief Executive Officer
The Walt Disney Company

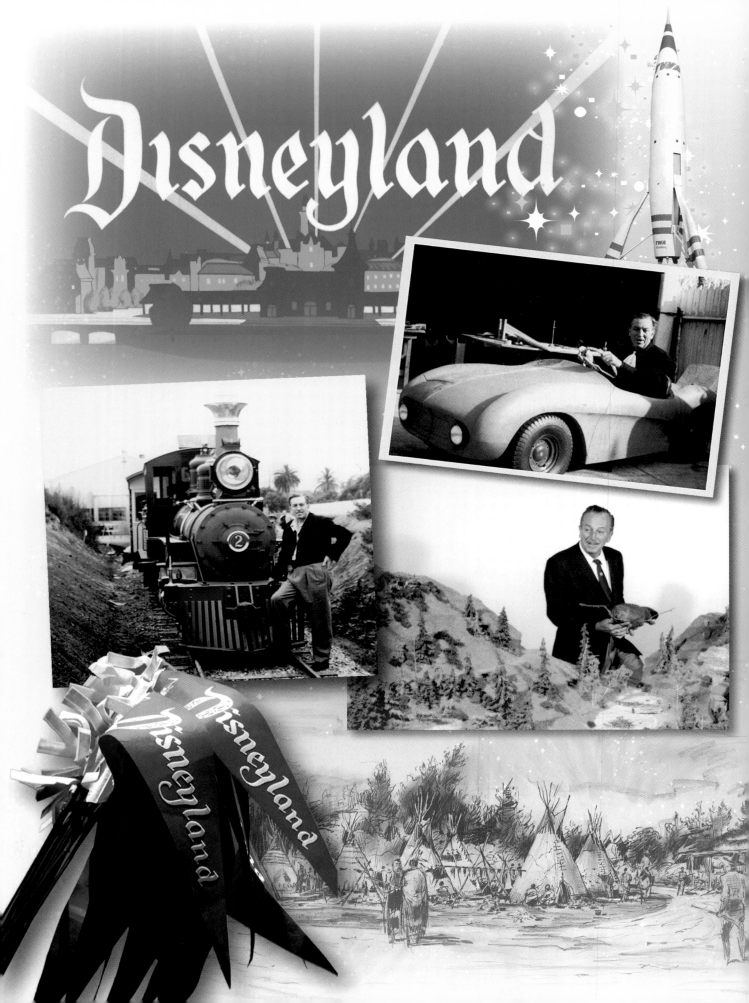

DREAMS

The Who, What, and "Walt" of Disneyland

Walt Disney believed in
the power of having a dream.

It has often been said that what
differentiated Walt Disney from other
men with big dreams was that he was both a dreamer
and a doer. Dreams of the past, of fantasy, adventure,
and the future all combined to create Walt's dream of
Disneyland and his personal persistence of vision made
his dream a reality.

"I think what I want Disneyland to be most of all is a happy
place—a place where adults and children can experience
together some of the wonders of life, of adventure, and feel
better because of it," Walt once commented.

So settle back and get ready to immerse yourself in one of the
greatest dreams of the twentieth century, a dream we all share,
a beloved dream that we can relive . . . then, now, and forever.

Walt Disney: The Man and the Company

Walt Disney didn't create Disneyland alone. Long before any ground was broken for the project and years before his valued "Imagineers" and "Cast Members" appeared on the scene, Walt only had two true partners in his desire to create "some sort of amusement enterprise"—his big brother Roy O. Disney (company co-founder and financial steward of Walt Disney Productions, now known as The Walt Disney Company) and the most popular animated film star of all time, Mickey Mouse.

From Walt's earliest notions about creating some sort of outdoor entertainment venue, and through its many different incarnations (studio tour, or a park near his studio, for example), the creative catalyst was always Mickey Mouse.

When Walt announced his plans for Disneyland during the premiere episode of his weekly television series (appropriately called *Disneyland*), he did so with Mickey at his side, reminding everyone "I only hope that we never lose sight of one thing—that it was all started by a mouse." After Disneyland opened in 1955, Mickey assumed the role of official host, and has faithfully welcomed over 500 million guests to "The Happiest Place on Earth."

However, behind Walt and Mickey stood Roy O. Disney, who had the hardest role to play, finding the money to support his younger brother's ever growing dream. Like everyone else, Roy was initially unsupportive of Walt's wild idea, but as with previous ventures, through his passion, enthusiasm, and excitement, Walt was able to win over Roy. With everyone predicting financial disaster and offering countless words of discouragement, Roy steadfastly stayed at his brother's side, eventually utilizing his financial genius to secure the funding to make Walt's dream a reality and, along with Mickey, create the world's very first Disney theme park.

LEFT: *A mountain of fan mail stands as testimony to the phenomenal popularity of Walt Disney and Mickey Mouse.*

OPPOSITE: *Walt and Roy Disney.*

ABOVE: *In the late 1940s, Walt Disney discovered an after-hours, stress-relieving secret—backyard railroading. He was formally introduced to the hobby by two of his top animators, Ward Kimball and Ollie Johnston (seen above with Walt). Walt's backyard railroad, headed up by a little steam engine dubbed the Lilly Belle, after Walt's wife Lillian, officially debuted on May 15, 1950, and became one of the key inspirations that led to the development of Disneyland.*

Walt's Dream of Disneyland

Following the 1937 premiere of *Snow White and the Seven Dwarfs* (the first successful feature-length animated film ever produced), Walt realized that his little studio on Hyperion Avenue in Los Angeles would no longer be able to handle his ambitious plans for more feature animated films. On August 31, 1938, the Disney brothers put down a deposit on 51 acres of land in Burbank, California, and began drawing up plans to build a state-of-the art animation film studio.

Once the final move into the new studio was completed on May 6, 1940, Walt held fast to his dream of creating some sort of an attraction the public could enjoy. "You know it's a shame people come to Hollywood and find there's nothing to see," Walt commented in the early 1940s. "Wouldn't it be nice if people could come to Hollywood and see something?"

Throughout the years the concept of Walt's dream took many forms, always rooted to a location at the Burbank studio. The project was unveiled in the March 27, 1952, edition of the

ABOVE: *This concept rendering by artist Harper Goff was created in 1951 and is considered to be the earliest visualization of a proposed park located on a 16-acre plot across the street from the Disney Studios in Burbank. The design for this "Mickey Mouse Park" was heavily influenced by a 1948 trip Walt made to Greenfield Village in Michigan, Henry Ford's museum honoring America's turn-of-the-century inventors.*

Burbank *Daily Review* with the headline: "WALT DISNEY MAKE-BELIEVE LAND PROJECT PLANNED HERE—$1.5 MILLION DREAMLAND TO RISE ON SITE IN BURBANK" and the article contained the first time the project was dubbed "Disneyland."

A colored pencil and watercolor rendering by artist Harper Goff visualized a 16-acre park across the street from the Walt Disney Studios, bordering the Los Angeles River, and featured red pencil notes indicating placements for a bird island, a steamboat, fairground and picnic areas, and, of course, a steam train.

Walt kept dreaming and developing his idea and soon it became apparent that the little plot of land couldn't contain everything he had in mind.

ABOVE: *The Walt Disney Studios in Burbank, seen in the 1950s. Superimposed to the right is Harper Goff's 1951 rendering, showing the proposed location of the original Disneyland along Riverside Drive. Today this site is home to Walt Disney Feature Animation and the West Coast headquarters for the ABC Television network—as well as a California freeway that runs right through the spot where the lake would have been.*

DISNEYLAND

SCHEMATIC AERIAL VIEW
APPROX. 45 ACRES
WITHIN RAILROAD TRACKS
DESIGNED BY WED ENTERPRISES

In December 1952, Walt Disney established W.E.D. Enterprises (WED, an acronym for Walter Elias Disney and now known as Walt Disney Imagineering), his privately held creative think tank chartered with creating Disneyland. The team of skilled writers, architects, draftsmen, artists, engineers, sculptors, and special-effects experts were dubbed "Imagineers." In the fall of 1953, Roy Disney had the unenviable job of going to New York City to try and sell his younger brother's big dream to the bankers. Unfortunately, he had nothing to show them. Nothing like Disneyland had ever been seen before, and Roy knew from experience that bankers were not an easy audience.

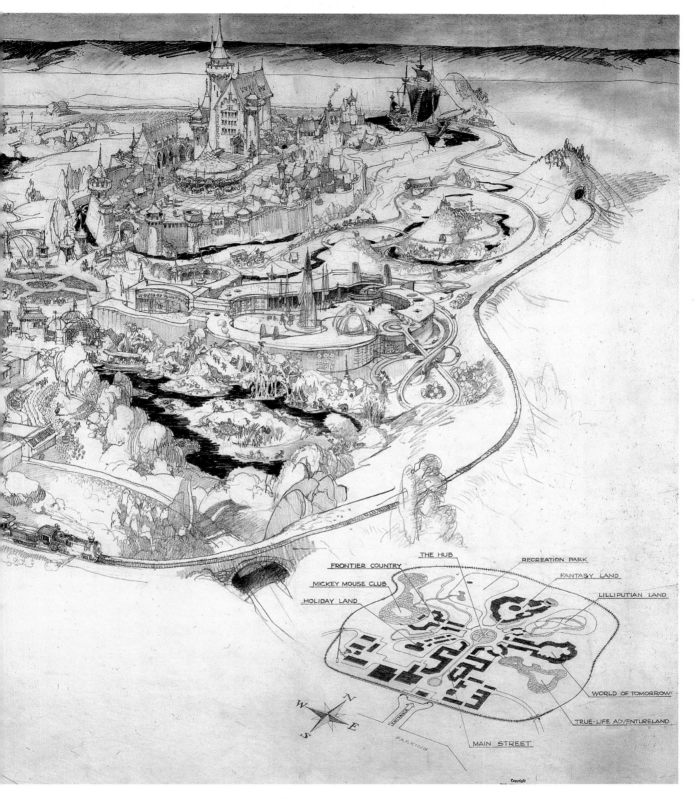

Walt admitted, "dreams offer too little collateral" to bankers. So over the weekend of September 23, 1953, Walt spent a marathon forty-eight hours at his studio with noted artist Herb Ryman creating the first true visualization of what we now recognize as Disneyland (above). The 43 x 70-inch pencil conceptual sketch, created under Walt's direct supervision, combined all of the disparate ideas that had been generated by the Imagineers, and presented a groundbreaking layout of five themed "lands" centered around a central plaza "hub."

Dreaming of the Past

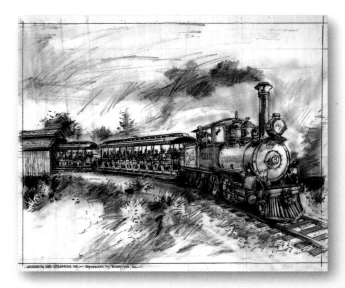

"I love the nostalgic myself," Walt Disney once said. "I hope we never lose some of the things of the past." Walt made good on his wish by incorporating Main Street, U.S.A., the gateway and main thoroughfare of the park, into the overall design of Disneyland. Inspired by Walt's childhood hometown of Marceline, Missouri, the Imagineers made sure that contemporary audiences would embrace and appreciate the charm and quaintness of this quintessential Main Street at the turn of the twentieth century, featuring gas lamps, hitching posts, gingerbread Victorian architecture, and horse-drawn streetcars.

TOP: *Rendering of the* Fred Gurley *excursion train along the Disneyland Railroad by Disney Imaginer Sam McKim.*

ABOVE: *An early concept sketch of Main Street, U.S.A., by Disney Imaginer Sam McKim that is remarkably accurate to the finished reality.*

LEFT: *1951 rendering of the office of* The Weekly Bugle *newspaper on Main Street by Disney Imagineer Harper Goff.*

BELOW: *1951 concept sketch of proposed "General Merchandise" establishment on Main Street, U.S.A.*

BOTTOM: *This 1955 rendering of Main Street, U.S.A., by Sam McKim is rare because it was based on a finalized set of architectural blueprints for the "Drug Store" and "Ice Cream Parlor." Soon after, architects would take their cue from the concept sketches of the Imagineers, not the other way around, a process that would become a unique hallmark of the Disney Imagineers.*

Dreaming of Fantasy

Fantasyland is often called the heart of Disneyland because it was primarily Disney's classic animated films and beloved characters that formed the basis for many of Walt's early concepts for the park. "In this timeless land of enchantment, the age of chivalry, magic, and make-believe are reborn," Walt Disney once stated. "Fantasyland is dedicated to the young and the young-in-heart."

THIS PAGE: *Disney artist Bruce Bushman created these early concept sketches for favorite Fantasyland attractions such as this early design concept for an attraction vehicle for Snow White's Scary Adventures (top). Concepts for the Mad Tea Party featured elaborate set pieces at the entrance and center of the attraction (middle). The medieval tournament tent motif of King Arthur Carrousel became the theme for all the Fantasyland architecture, showcased in this early concept sketch (above).*

THIS PAGE: *Disney artist Bruce Bushman also created these concepts for three popular Fantasyland attractions including Dumbo the Flying Elephant (top), Storybook Land Canal Boats (middle; featuring a fun-filled chute where guests would ride down the tongue of Monstro the Whale), and Casey Jr. Circus Train (bottom).*

Inspired by his popular *True-Life Adventure* nature documentaries of the 1950s and early 1960s, Adventureland was Walt's way of creating a microcosm of many of the world's far-off places and uncharted regions. Walt envisioned Frontierland in much the same manner, as a salute to the romance and spirit of the American West. In each of these realms, would-be explorers in khaki shorts, or modern-day pioneers in sneakers and coonskin caps could live out their wildest dreams . . . dreams filled with danger, mystery, and courage.

Dreaming of Adventure

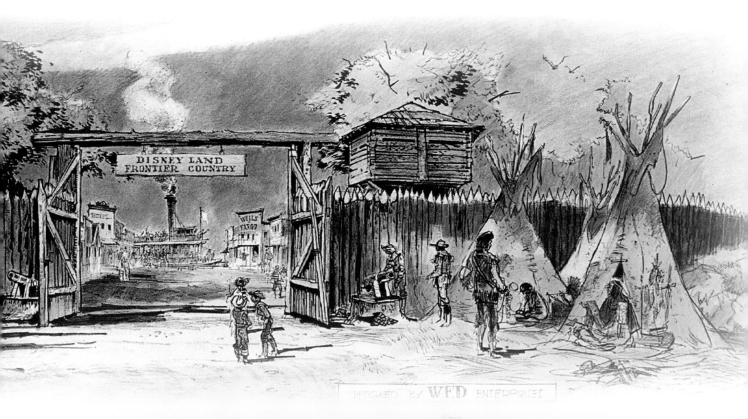

TOP: *Artist Herbert Ryman's elaborate concept sketch depicting how the entrance to Frontierland would mimic an authentic western stockade typical of the American frontier (note the name "Frontier Country" over the entryway).*

LEFT: *1956 rendering highlighting the Cantina and Mineral Hall in Frontierland, by Disney Imagineer Sam McKim.*

ABOVE: *Disney Imagineer Harper Goff illustrates the elevation of an "ancient" Cambodian shrine along the banks of the Jungle Cruise in this 1954 rendering.*

Dreaming of the Future

In creating his original vision of "Tomorrow" in 1955, Walt showed people what the world would look like in the far-off year of 1986!

"A vista into a world of wondrous ideas, signifying man's achievements . . . a step into the future, with predictions of constructive things to come," is how Walt described Tomorrowland. However, in the Cold War era of 1955, Tomorrowland offered much more than a respite into a mechanized future, it truly offered hope and optimism for a unified world filled with rockets, flying spacemen, sleek monorails, and nuclear-powered submarines.

ABOVE: *Walt surveys a model of the moon in preparation for his Rocket to the Moon attraction.*

BACKGROUND: *Disney Imagineer Herb Ryman created the 1954 rendering of Tomorrowland, prominently featuring the Moonliner Rocket, and far in the distance the Clock of the World, which told the time anywhere on the Planet Earth.*

TOP: *Chromed monorails criss-cross over Tomorrowland in this 1959 rendering by Disney Imagineer John Hench.*

ABOVE: *The train of tomorrow—the Viewliner, one of the shortest-lived attractions at Disneyland (1957–1958) is seen in this 1957 concept rendering by Disney Imagineer Sam McKim.*

What was there before
DISNEYLAND

SANTA ANA FREEWAY

HARBOR BLVD.

FUTURE SITE OF
DISNEYLAND CITY HALL

ADVENTURELAND

After Walt's initial proposal of locating Disneyland on sixteen acres of studio property in Burbank fell through, he hired the Stanford Research Institute in 1953 to find the best possible site for his park. SRI recommended the wide-open spaces of Anaheim in Orange County, California, just 27 miles south of downtown Los Angeles. (Today the actual geo-population center of Southern California is a mere four miles from Disneyland.) The road seen crossing through the center of this aerial photo is the under-construction Santa Ana Freeway, with Harbor Boulevard branching off to the right. The clump of trees at the extreme right center of the photo would establish the location of Adventureland, which had originally been planned for the opposite side of the Park. Those trees remain to this day.

FANTASYLAND

TOMORROWLAND

FRONTIERLAND

MAIN STREET

ADVENTURELAND

CITY HALL

    In August 1953, one hundred sixty acres of orange groves and walnut trees, comprised of
parcels owned by seventeen different families, were selected as the future home of Disneyland.
The subsequent land purchase was kept quiet until the news broke on May 1, 1954, by the
Anaheim Bulletin newspaper. Walt wanted to keep as many of the site's existing trees as possible,
so each tree was tagged with a different colored ribbon to indicate "move," "remove," or "save."
To Walt's dismay, most of the trees were bulldozed—the bulldozer operator was color-blind!
However, the giant eucalpytus trees seen in the exact center of this image (the same ones
identified in the image opposite) were saved, and today serve as a backdrop for the Jungle Cruise
in Adventureland. Also visible in this image are the homes of the original landowners, many of
which were relocated behind Main Street and used to house the Disneyland administrators.
Ron Dominguez, the son of one of those landowners, who would go on to become executive
vice-president of Disneyland, was born in one of those houses!

ABOVE: *By October 15, 1954, the elevated dirt berm that surrounds the park is taking shape, and the "Rivers of America" is clearly visible toward the bottom of this aerial photo. Near the right center of the image, planting has begun in the jungles of Adventureland.*

RIGHT: *The beginnings of Fantasyland, seen in December 1954. The L-shaped building at the top will soon be home to Snow White, with Peter Pan and Mr. Toad in the lower building. Sleeping Beauty Castle will soon unite the two structures to form the Fantasyland courtyard.*

BELOW: *In the early months of 1955, all the major landmarks of the Park are visible, except for Tomorrowland. Due to a shortage of time, money, and resources, construction on the land of the future had been delayed, and would not begin until a few months before the Park opened.*

What was the first building built at Disneyland?

The very first completed building at Disneyland was the Opera House on Main Street. Today, the Opera House is home to "Great Moments with Mr. Lincoln," but up until 1960 it housed the Disneyland Mill, where all the intricate woodwork throughout the Park was produced.

ABOVE: *Main Street under construction. The freestanding white concrete walls at the bottom left of this image are the tunnels that would soon lead guests under the railroad tracks and into Walt's Magic Kingdom. The elevated dirt berm built to support the tracks (and to screen Disneyland from the outside world) is visible to the left and right of the tunnels. Also visible at the upper left is the stand of eucalyptus trees identified in the aerial photos on pages 16 and 17. Directly across from the trees on the bottom right is the framework for the Opera House.*

MIDDLE: *The almost-completed Opera House in Town Square.*

RIGHT: *Interior of the Opera House, in use as the Disneyland wood mill.*

ABOVE: *Legendary Disney art director Harper Goff (with hand on hip) oversees the intricate rockwork textures of Schweitzer Falls, at the heart of the Jungle Cruise.*

MIDDLE: *Monstro the Whale takes shape in steel and fiberglass. Note the broken pieces that have been removed and are being resculpted at the request of the art director.*

BELOW: *The Disneyland Opera House gets its front facade.*

A Dream Comes True
OPENING DAY

From July 21, 1954, to Opening Day, the actual building of Disneyland had consumed over 2 million board feet of lumber; a million square feet of asphalt was laid; 5,000 cubic yards of concrete poured; 35,000 cubic yards of dirt moved to create the park's surrounding earthen berm; and virtually every nursery from Santa Barbara to San Diego was depleted in an effort to complete the park's landscaping. Work on the park continued right up to the morning of opening day.

On Sunday, July 17, 1955, history was made. Disneyland, the very first Disney theme park and the groundbreaking masterpiece that has been the cloth from which all other Disney theme parks and resorts through the years have been cut, officially opened to the world.

At two o'clock that afternoon the gates of Disneyland opened. Ten thousand special guests had been invited. But by day's end, 33,000 people had packed the park for the opening day invitation was so prized that counterfeit tickets proliferated. Attractions broke down. There was a power outage in Fantasyland, restaurants ran out of food, and the freshly poured asphalt on Main Street was so soft that it stole the high-heeled shoes right off many a female guest. The day would forever after be known in Disney lore as "Black Sunday."

However, the greatest souvenir of Black Sunday is the kinescope of the live ABC Television broadcast of the opening day festivities. Covered by 29 cameras, the show was the most elaborate live TV broadcast produced to that point in time (three cameras were the norm), viewed by an estimated audience of 90 million. Hosted by TV stars Art Linkletter, Bob Cummings, and Ronald Reagan, the show was full of gaffes and snafus, but the inherent sense of fun and buoyant excitement everyone exhibits makes it a treasured part of the Disney legacy.

OPPOSITE LEFT: *Walt Disney rehearses his dedication of Disneyland.*

ABOVE: *California Governor Goodwin Knight speaks at the dedication ceremonies. Other celebrities in attendance included Fess Parker, Buddy Ebsen, and the Mouseketeers.*

BELOW: *A never-before-seen panoramic view of the dedication ceremonies in Town Square.*

TRADITIONS

Endearing Sights, Sounds, and Special Occasions

Traditions are an integral part of the magic of Disneyland because they ensure a timeless quality to every visit. Beloved Disneyland traditions, from marching bands on Main Street to cast member name tags, have been passed down from one generation to the next, while new traditions are continually introduced.

A visit to Disneyland has itself become a yearly family tradition for many, not unlike celebrating Thanksgiving, Halloween, or the Fourth of July. As the world constantly changes, there are aspects of Disneyland that have remained constant, becoming endearing sights, sounds, and occasions that add to the charm of "The Happiest Place on Earth."

WALT

Disneyland
103

Board the
SANTA FE
& DISNEYLAND R.R.
at Main St.
Frontierland
or Fantasyland depots

SANTA FE & D

MAIN STREET

The Traditions of MAIN STREET

Main Street, U.S.A., abounds with Disneyland traditions. Inspired in part by Walt Disney's boyhood hometown of Marceline, Missouri, Main Street represents small town American life at the turn of the twentieth century. However, over the years Main Street has evolved to become an idealized version of everyone's hometown—regardless of age or background everyone can relate to the warmth, charms, and welcoming spirit of Main Street.

From the familiar flowering face of Mickey Mouse in front of the Main Street Train Station to the nostalgic songs of the Dapper Dans barbershop quartet, Main Street is the one area of Disneyland that has physically changed the least over the past fifty years.

One Main Street tradition can trace its origins back to Opening Day in 1955. The popular Disneyland Band is a Main Street staple, logging well over 3,500 marching miles and more than 75,000 performances. The band currently boasts a repertoire of more than 400 tunes.

Main Street is also known for its whimsical and ornate second-story window advertisements. In addition to decor, the windows serve the function of honoring key Disney Cast Members, Imagineers, and artists who have left an indelible mark on Disneyland. The tradition of showcasing "Disneylanders" with such an honor goes back to Walt Disney himself, who paid tribute to his father with a window over the Main Street Emporium: "Elias Disney, Contractor, Est. 1895" (the elder Disney was actually a building contractor in Chicago).

OPPOSITE: *The original color artwork created for the opening sequence of the Disneyland television show.*

ABOVE: *The tradition of the Disneyland Band, seen in this 1960s view of Main Street, U.S.A.*

ABOVE: *From 1963 to 1964, the Opera House became the "Mickey Mouse Club Headquarters" where children could sign up and get their own official membership cards in the Mickey Mouse Club.*

LEFT: *During the holiday season of 1961, the Opera House was finally utilized as an attraction when Walt Disney had the sets from his big-screen musical film* Babes in Toyland *transplanted to Disneyland. Here, Bo Peep and trees from the "Forest of No Return" entertain a pair of special visitors.*

BELOW: *The actual set of "Mother Goose Village" from the film* Babes in Toyland.

ABOVE: *The Four Freedoms Mural once graced the exit area from Great Moments with Mr. Lincoln.*

RIGHT: *On July 18, 1965, Great Moments With Mr. Lincoln premiered at the Main Street Opera House.*

BELOW RIGHT: *Today, Mr. Lincoln delivers his famed "Gettysburg Address."*

BELOW: *Disneyland is the only Disney park to feature an Opera House on its Main Street.*

OPERA HOUSE

Hear Lincoln Speak
The Gettysburg Address
Great Moments with Mr. Lincoln

THE WALT DISNEY STORY
FEATURING GREAT MOMENTS WITH MR. LINCOLN

TOP AND ABOVE: *The annual Candlelight Procession celebrates the holiday season.*

A Tradition in Candlelight

Two of the most beloved Main Street traditions take place in the cozy warmth of Town Square, home to many memorable Disneyland special occasions.

Established in 1958, the Disneyland Candlelight Procession is perhaps the most dramatic and compelling holiday celebration presented in the Park. Featuring church, high school, and college choirs from throughout Southern California, the impressive procession of carolers leaves Sleeping Beauty Castle and proceeds down Main Street, which is illuminated only by the hand-held tapers of the singers. The finale of the procession occurs in Town Square, when the choirs assemble in front of the Main Street Station and, accompanied by a live orchestra, join a special guest narrator in telling the traditional Christmas story in song and word. Through the years, such respected performers as James Earl Jones, Edward James Olmos, Lou Gossett, Jr., John Wayne, Cary Grant, and Charlton Heston have lent their narrative skills to this remarkable presentation.

Town Square also plays host to the afternoon flag retreat ceremony, featuring the Disneyland Band. Activity on Main Street ceases as the "Star Spangled Banner" is played. This stirring ceremony elicits attention from all onlookers, from the misty veteran to parents teaching their children to stand at attention as a sign of respect for the flag.

ABOVE: *The Disneyland Band assembles in Town Square for the patriotic late-afternoon flag retreat ceremony.*

A Tradition of
COSTUMES

Like in any theatrical presentation, the "on-stage" employees ("Cast Members" in Disney-speak) of Disneyland are appropriately costumed to convincingly play their "roles" in the Disneyland "show." Since the early years of the park, costumes have played an integral part in visually communicating the various themes and time periods represented throughout the eight themed "lands" of Disneyland.

The tradition of properly costuming the Disneyland cast continues to this day, with an inventory of over 800,000 garments for over 15,000 Cast Members and 650 Audio-Animatronics performers. Over 20,000 costume pieces are exchanged per week for cleaning during the peak summer months, with approximately 100,000 items repaired each year. The average life of each operational costume can be between nine months and five years.

Everything from the casual and comfortable attire of the Main Gate Cast Members to the elaborate and detailed costumes of the Park's various parades and shows (plus everything in-between for the attractions, shops, and restaurants) is designed and created at the Disneyland Resort by a specialized team of designers, tailors, buyers, coordinators, and administrators.

Every new costume takes eight to twelve months to create, from initial sketch to final product. Disneyland stocks 500,000 yards of material annually, covering 900 different kinds of fabric. Costume designs are constantly re-evaluated and updated to reflect new fabrics, durability, and comfort considerations, plus the effectiveness of how well each costume conveys its respective theme.

LEFT: *One of the earliest (and most unusual) Disneyland costumes was worn by the balloon sellers on Main Street in the 1950s.*

TOP RIGHT: *In 1959, these costumes made piloting the monorail one of the most sought-after positions at Disneyland.*

RIGHT: *The colorful Alpine costume of Matterhorn Mountain, circa 1964.*

THIS PAGE: *Disneyland costumes from the late 1950s to the present day. Clockwise from top left: Main Street Plaza Pavilion, Tom Sawyer Island rafts, Fantasyland foods, Matterhorn Mountain, Adventure Thru Inner Space, and the Toontown Jolly Trolley.*

A Tradition of
TICKET BOOKS

When the Park opened in 1955 Disneyland offered individual tickets for each attraction. The concept of "Ticket Books" was introduced on October 11, 1955, with the "Day at Disneyland" book. This first ticket book consisted of park admission as well as "A," "B," and "C" tickets, each featuring various attractions (total cost for an adult: $2.50). Over the years, as more attractions were added to the Park, more tickets were added to the books. The "D" ticket first appeared in 1956, and the famous "E" ticket was added in 1959 with the opening of such classic Disneyland attractions as the Submarine Voyage, Monorail, and Matterhorn Bobsleds.

In 1982, the ticket books were retired after the introduction of the Disneyland Passport, which granted admission to the Park and all its attractions.

Through the years leftover tickets and ticket books, which never expired, were saved by guests of all ages for use on their next visit or kept as souvenirs. Today, vintage Disneyland ticket books are among the more popular Disneyland collectibles.

ABOVE: *Disneyland Admission Ticket #1, purchased by Roy O. Disney, in a show of faith for his brother's dream.*
BACKGROUND: *The back cover of "A Day at Disneyland," the first ticket book, introduced in October 1955.*

BELOW: *The most famous ticket of all: the very first "E" ticket, introduced in 1959. Through the years the "E" came to represent what were considered the best or most thrilling Disneyland attractions, prompting U.S. astronaut Sally Ride to exclaim, after ascending into space aboard the space shuttle in 1986, "That's a real 'E'-Ticket ride!"*

BOTTOM: *The first Disneyland Ticket Book, introduced in October 1955, featured only "A," "B," and "C" tickets. As the Park expanded over the years, "D" tickets and then "E" tickets were added to the mix.*

A Tradition of
MEMORIES

A visit to Disneyland is always exciting, and for some Park guests a fond reminder of the magic of Disneyland goes home with them at the end of the day—in the form of a souvenir book or via fanciful postcards shared with friends and family.

With the creation of the very first Disneyland souvenir guidebook in 1955 a tradition was born—the annual publication of colorful, richly illustrated keepsakes of trips to "The Happiest Place on Earth." These books initially served as helpful references for a day at the Park, but through the years they have evolved to become treasured collectibles. Each souvenir book reflects the decade in which it was published, inspiring return visits or captivating the imaginations of people who have never been.

Like the popular souvenir books, postcards from Disneyland have also evolved, becoming highly sought-after collectibles. Each postcard is a snapshot of its time. Since the Park opened, more than a thousand different Disneyland postcard designs have been produced and mailed to every corner of the world.

ABOVE: *The 1955 Disneyland Guidebook went to press before the Park was finished, and so contained only artists' renderings.*

RIGHT TOP: *The 1956 Guidebook.*

RIGHT BOTTOM: *The 1960 Guidebook, featuring the first "E"-Ticket attractions.*

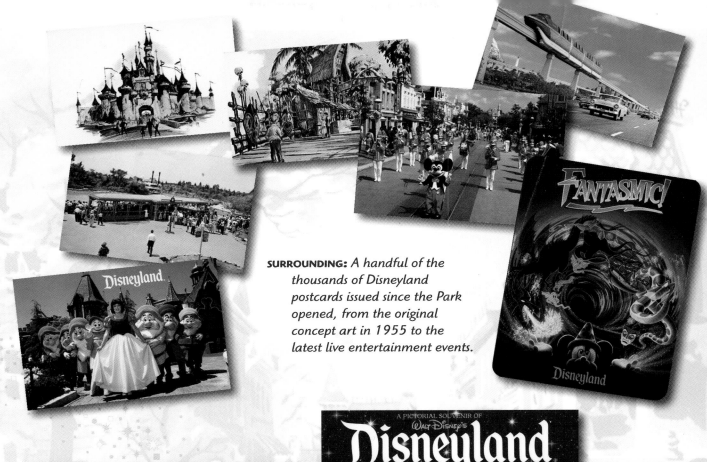

SURROUNDING: *A handful of the thousands of Disneyland postcards issued since the Park opened, from the original concept art in 1955 to the latest live entertainment events.*

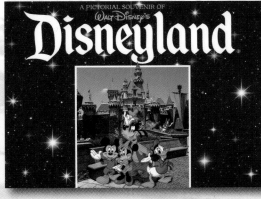

ABOVE: *Guidebooks from the first five decades of Disneyland, each one filled with the memories, the look, the styling, and the feelings of its era.*

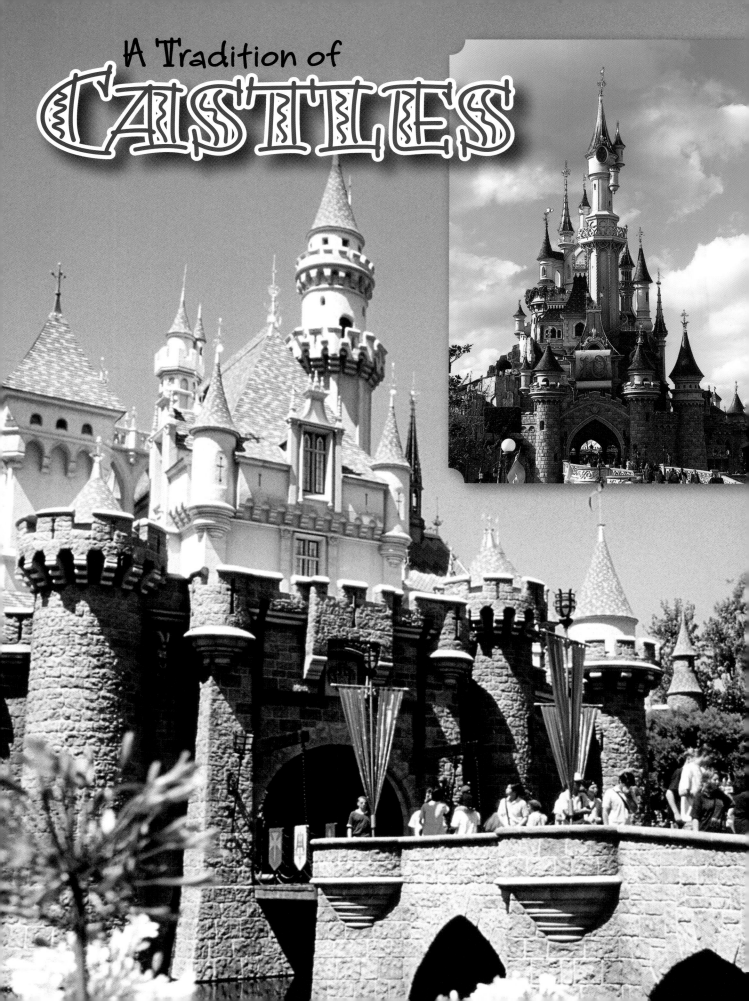

A Tradition of CASTLES

Sleeping Beauty Castle was established long before either Disneyland or the animated feature from which it was derived. The castle began as part of the opening titles for the *Disneyland* TV series in 1954 and, along with Tinker Bell, went on to "welcome" viewers to various Disney TV shows.

In the early design stages of Disneyland it was determined that a castle gateway to Fantasyland would also act as the central visual icon or "anchor" for the Park. Thus was born one of Disney's most enduring symbols and the tradition of making a castle the focal point of each Magic Kingdom around the world.

Sharp eyes will notice details such as the Disney family crest above the entrance, 22-karat gold-leafing adorning the spires, "squirrel" water spouts inspired by Princess Aurora's woodland friends, and hand-rendered fresco paintings depicting scenes from the Disney film *Sleeping Beauty*. The castle also has a real functioning drawbridge (used only twice—on opening day and the rededication of Fantasyland in 1983).

Sleeping Beauty Castle is the smallest of all the Disney castles, perfectly matching the intimate scale of Disneyland. However, the Castle appears much taller than its 77-foot height through the use of a movie set-building technique called "forced perspective." The walls and battlements are constructed of "stones" sculpted in graduated sizes from large ones at the foundation to small ones at the turrets, thus tricking the eye into thinking the structure is actually much larger.

OPPOSITE: *Sleeping Beauty Castle at Disneyland.*

INSET OPPOSITE: *Le Château de la Belle au Bois Dormant at Disneyland Resort Paris.*

ABOVE TOP AND BOTTOM: *Cinderella Castle at Walt Disney World (top) and at Tokyo Disneyland (bottom).*

SURPRISES

Around every corner
when you least expect them!

The element of surprise plays a big role in the charm of Disneyland. Around virtually every corner guests may encounter a fantastic parade, spectacular fireworks, hidden delights, amazing sights, and unexpected chance meetings. Over the years some "surprises" have come and gone, while others remain to delight guests again and again—all part of the magic of Disneyland.

Unexpected Delights

LEFT: *From 1957 to 1964 Disneyland guests "flipped" over the annual "Western National Pancake Races" held on Main Street, U.S.A. where housewives raced down Main Street trying to flip pancakes over a suspended ribbon in record time.*

BELOW: *Guests to Disneyland in the summer of 1992 were surprised to find that after twilight the banks of the Rivers of America in Frontierland were magically transformed into a gigantic amphitheater for one of the most spectacular and popular shows in Disneyland history—Fantasmic!*

OPPOSITE LEFT: *In October 2004, some of America's Olympic champions did something no one has ever done before— swim down Main Street, U.S.A.! The full-length Olympic pool measured 21 feet wide and stretched almost the entire length of Main Street.*

RIGHT AND ABOVE RIGHT: *In celebration of its 35th anniversary, Disneyland presented the "Party Gras Parade," a confetti-filled "carnivale" set to pulsating Latin rhythms, with five gigantic inflatable balloon floats featuring Mickey, Minnie, Donald, Pluto, and Goofy—each towering a spectacular 45 feet high.*

BACKGROUND: *On December 5, 1985, the city of Anaheim produced a gala salute to 30 years of Disneyland by presenting Skyfest, a world-record-breaking release of millions of colorful balloons over "The Happiest Place on Earth."*

THE MICKEY MOUSE CLUB CIRCUS

Tucked away in Fantasyland (on the site of the future Motor Boat Cruise), the Mickey Mouse Club Circus starred many of the performers from the popular Mickey Mouse Club television show, including the Mouseketeers as stunt riders and trapeze artists, plus head Mouseketeers Jimmie Dodd and Roy Williams. The concept of a circus appealed to Walt because he could recall childhood memories of majestic parades with exotic animals whenever the circus came to his hometown. Everything about the Mickey Mouse Club Circus was on an impressive scale: a daily parade, seating for 2,500 guests in two tents, and the longest show in Disneyland history at 75 minutes. But guests at Disneyland were more interested in seeing the Park than a circus, even a snazzy Disney version. Following its premiere performance on November 24, 1955, the circus folded its tent on January 8, 1956, and paraded back into Disneyland history.

ABOVE: *Walt poses with Serenado the Wonder Horse (one of the stars of the circus), along with his trainers.*

RIGHT: *Similar to attractions in the Park, individual tickets for the Mickey Mouse Club Circus could be purchased at nearby little kiosks.*

TOP: *The entrance to the Mickey Mouse Club Circus.*

MIDDLE: *The wide-open spaces of Anaheim can be seen behind the striped tent of the Mickey Mouse Club Circus.*

BOTTOM: *Authentic circus wagons were featured as decor at the entrance to the circus tent.*

MAX   BUFF   MELVIN

Keeping in Character

LEFT: *For almost three decades, Max, Buff, and Melvin presided over the Country Bear Jamboree. Today, the Jamboree is gone...but its favorite threesome still presides over...well, that's the surprise. Keep your eyes open!*

RIGHT: *In 1988, Big Thunder Ranch in Frontierland greeted a new resident—Mickey Moo, a cow who sported a naturally occurring silhouette of Mickey Mouse. Moo became quite an attraction and "milked" guests for attention as well as hay.*

BELOW: *The presidential elections of 1972 and 1976 featured a unique candidate who ran on the campaign promise of "honey in every pot" during Winnie the Pooh for President Days, featuring rousing, tongue-in-cheek rallies in Town Square.*

RIGHT: *Debuting with the Submarine Voyage in 1959, the mermaids made such a "splash" that they returned in 1965. Unfortunately, the chlorine used in the water consistently bleached their wavy locks a bright yellowish green, and overzealous men, who couldn't resist their appeal, occasionally jumped in the lagoon to get a closer look. In 1967 the Submarine Lagoon mermaids submerged into Disneyland history.*

LEFT AND ABOVE: *The classic imagery of Tinker Bell igniting fireworks over the Castle first began in 1954 with the debut of the Disneyland TV series. In 1961 Tinker Bell began appearing live at Disneyland, launching the Fantasy in the Sky fireworks. Tinker Bell's flight path over Fantasyland is 784 feet long, and begins at the 147-foot-tall Matterhorn Mountain. From there she glides effortlessly downward at air speeds of 15 miles per hour.*

ABOVE LEFT: *In 1986 Disneyland guests encountered a bizarre crew of intergalactic refugees in Tomorrowland—Major Domo, Hooter, and Idee and Odee from the 3–D spectacular* Captain EO.

ABOVE RIGHT: *In the autumn of 1987 and 1988, Disneyland held a "State Fair," a country–fair–inspired event that featured an abundance of funnel cake, turkey legs, log–rolling competitions, and a gigantic Ferris wheel. Among the highlights were the daily Pig Races at Big Thunder Ranch, where standing–room–only audiences went "hog wild" over the white–knuckle competition of the little "hams."*

BELOW: *The Gift–Giver Extraordinaire Machine premiered at the Main Gate during the 30th anniversary of Disneyland in 1985, counting up to the 250–millionth guest to enter the Park. Every 30th guest received a prize, with the more elaborate prizes (including a brand–new car every day) eliciting a spray of confetti and boisterous horns and sirens.*

BELOW: *Disneyland turned back the clock and saluted the fabulous '50s and early '60s with Blast to the Past, a popular springtime event presented in 1988 and 1989.*

BOTTOM: *Travelers down Harbor Boulevard in 1989 were surprised to find two Disneyland marquees standing side by side, as the fifth (and final) incarnation was being installed. The Disneyland sign made its debut in 1958—there was no marquee for the first three years! The sign was a local icon until the last one came down on June 14, 1999 to make room for the expanded Disneyland Resort.*

Peter Pan

Enjoy the exciting adventures of
SNOW WHITE
PETER PAN
MR. TOAD

Fantasyland

Explore Unchart
SUBMARINE VOYA
thru liquid space

TOMORROWLAI

STAGE COACH RIDE

DISNEYLAND STAGE LINES

MINE TRAIN RIDE

MULE PACK RIDE

FRONTIERLAND

mind thy head

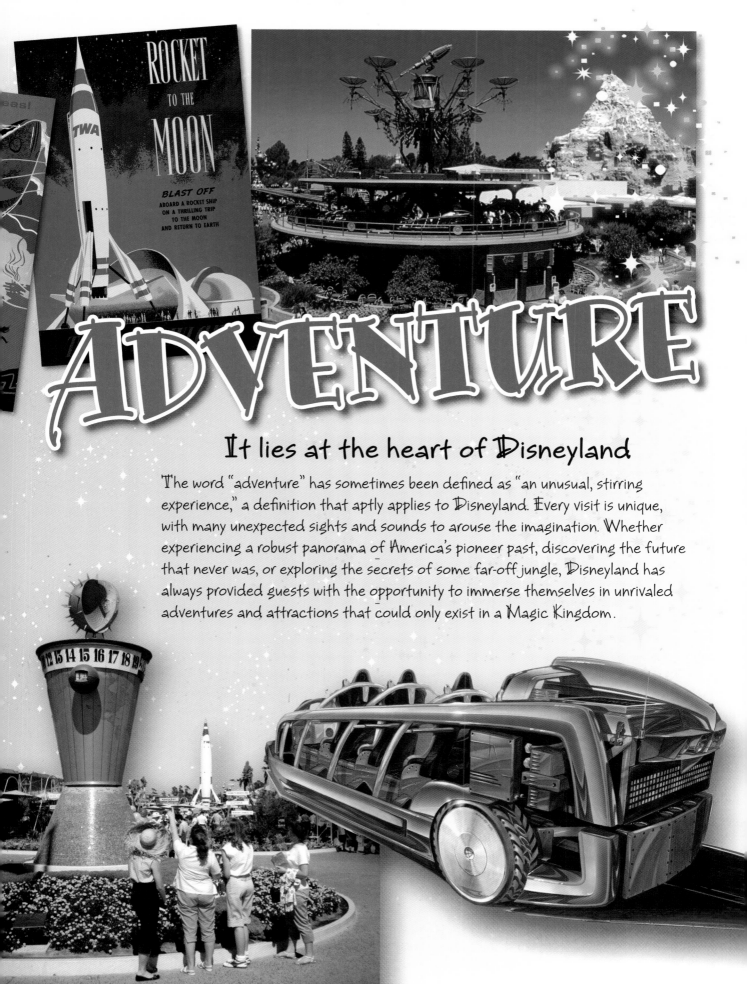

ADVENTURE

It lies at the heart of Disneyland

The word "adventure" has sometimes been defined as "an unusual, stirring experience," a definition that aptly applies to Disneyland. Every visit is unique, with many unexpected sights and sounds to arouse the imagination. Whether experiencing a robust panorama of America's pioneer past, discovering the future that never was, or exploring the secrets of some far-off jungle, Disneyland has always provided guests with the opportunity to immerse themselves in unrivaled adventures and attractions that could only exist in a Magic Kingdom.

Adventures in the Future
TOMORROWLAND

Walt Disney's peek into the future, Tomorrowland, has been described many ways through the years. "A vista into a world of wondrous ideas, signifying man's achievements...a step into the future, with predictions of constructive things to come...a world on the move...a future that never was...imagination and beyond."

When Disneyland opened, Tomorrowland was the least complete portion of the park. Nonetheless, this first incarnation of Tomorrowland quickly developed its own unique charms, presenting the future as predicted for the year 1986 (significant for the return of Halley's Comet), with "atomic-era" design influences, such as "googie" architecture, a Moonliner Rocket, a Hall of Chemistry, the Bathroom of Tomorrow, and wide open "Autopia" freeways of the future.

By the mid 1960s the march of time and progress had caught up to Tomorrowland, with many of its predictions for the future—satellites, nuclear power, freeways, and annual space missions—all having become a reality. So Walt Disney commissioned the creation of a "new" Tomorrowland, featuring "A World on the Move" filled with PeopleMovers, a Carousel of Progress, and Adventure Thru Inner Space. This new version of Tomorrowland debuted on July 2, 1967, and promoted an optimistic view of the future, as exemplified by the fondly remembered song "Great Big Beautiful Tomorrow"—the signature tune of the Carousel of Progress attraction.

However, time does not stand still, not even for Disneyland, and by the early 1990s Tomorrowland once again seemed destined to fall into a state of retro kitsch. The conundrum of keeping ahead of progress was solved by creating "The Future That Never Was," as evidenced in the all-new Tomorrowland that premiered on May 22, 1998. With a swirling Astro Orbitor, racing Rocket Rods, and a fun-filled Imagination Institute, guests to Tomorrowland entered a whole new world of "Imagination and Beyond."

OPPOSITE: *The Moonliner Rocket looms 76 feet high over the new Flight Circle and Hobbyland in Tomorrowland in 1956.*

THEN AND NOW
TOMORROWLAND
1956

LEFT: *Guests traversed the colorful Avenue of Flags as they entered Tomorrowland in 1956. The giant Clock of the World (behind the American flag) displayed the correct time (down to the minute) anywhere in the world.*

TOP: *The Flight Circle featured demonstrations of model airplanes, race cars, and speedboats. In the distance are the wide open spaces of Anaheim, circa 1956.*

ABOVE: *Upon entering Tomorrowland in 1955 guests could enjoy such exhibits as Circarama, the Hall of Chemistry, the Hall of Aluminum Fame, and the Bathroom of Tomorrow.*

Tomorrowland 1967

ABOVE: *Tomorrowland 1967 was indeed "A World on the Move," with Skyway buckets, a PeopleMover, and monorails gliding overhead, while the vessels of the Submarine Voyage explored the depths of liquid space. The Disneyland Monorail was the first daily-operating monorail in the Western Hemisphere, while the PeopleMover was the first system of its kind in the United States.*

OPPOSITE TOP: *The entrance to the "new" Tomorrowland, under construction in 1967.*

OPPOSITE BOTTOM: *The steel structure of the PeopleMover station rises in the center of Tomorrowland.*

TOMORROWLAND TODAY

The newest version of Tomorrowland represents the worlds of imagination, discovery, and wonder, inspired by classic futurists such as Jules Verne, H.G. Wells, and Leonardo da Vinci, and modern visionaries such as Walt Disney and George Lucas. Tomorrowland now features a patina of muted burgundy, green, and purple, enhanced with neon, and a landscaping design of blooming edible plants including oranges, lemons, and cabbage.

ABOVE: *The kinetic sculpture of the Astro Orbitor, the modern-day incarnation of the original Astro-Jets.*

INSET: *The "AgriFuture" edible landscape and plant life.*

TOP: *Buzz Lightyear himself joins forces with Tomorrowland guests for the 50th Anniversary celebration.*

MIDDLE: *Each vehicle is equipped with laser guns to help "Space Scouts" battle the minions of the nefarious Emperor Zurg.*

BOTTOM: *Inside Buzz Lightyear Astro Blasters, the newest attraction in Tomorrowland.*

Adventures in ADVENTURELAND

Just beyond a small footbridge at the end of Main Street lies a mysterious world of dense jungles, exotic bazaars, and daring adventures. Originally based on Walt Disney's *True-Life Adventure* film series, Adventureland was conceived as a land of reality inside a world of fantasy, where Disneyland guests would encounter live animals and fact-filled jungle journeys. The live animals never inhabited the jungle, but the thrills that lie in store are as real as they can be.

OPPOSITE INSET: *The elephant bathing pool (where everyone is wearing their "trunks"), one of the sights along the Jungle Cruise.*

LEFT TOP: *For many years, the Safari Shooting Gallery utilized real pellets, requiring the maintenance teams to repaint the targets every night.*

LEFT MIDDLE: *Passengers aboard one of the original candy-striped Jungle Cruise boats.*

BOTTOM: *One of the new, more realistic looking Jungle Cruise boats introduced in the 1990s narrowly avoids a free shower.*

TreeTop Adventures

LEFT: The Swiss Family Treehouse was modeled after the tree-top home of the Robinson family from Walt Disney's classic film Swiss Family Robinson (1960).

BOTTOM: The 60-foot-tall tree (Latin name: Disneydendron semperflorens grandis for "large, everblooming Disney tree") opened on November 18, 1962, sporting 300,000 bright-red vinyl leaves. However, the red leaves quickly faded and were soon replaced with a more stable green vinyl.

RIGHT: *The concrete-covered steel limbs of the Treehouse extend 80 feet into the air (and its "roots" extend 40 feet into the ground).*

ABOVE AND RIGHT: *In honor of the Disney animated feature Tarzan, the Treehouse welcomed all new tenants, and new "stylized" leaves that matched the look of the film. In tribute to the tree's previous occupants, guests can still hear the familiar strains of the "Swisskapolka" song being played on an old gramophone.*

Adventures in
FRONTIERLAND

Walking across the entrance stockade into Frontierland, guests instantly encounter an impressive vista filled with iconic imagery that recalls America's legendary westward expansion—from a bustling riverfront of the 1700s to the parched southwest of the 1880s. Through the years guests have experienced a series of memorable Western adventures, including burro rides, a not-too-timely stagecoach, a mine train into the farthest reaches of the wilderness, and a breathtaking excursion through red-rock buttes.

TOP: *The Mark Twain Riverboat debuted with the Park on Opening Day in 1955. Its 105-foot-long hull was constructed at Todd Shipyards in San Pedro, California, with the superstructure built on the soundstages of the Walt Disney Studios in Burbank, California.*

ABOVE: *With its clapboard sidewalks, hitching posts, and dry goods store, Frontierland is the picture of "Western" culture.*

LEFT: *The rich Western landscape helps tell the story of Frontierland.*

THEN AND NOW
FRONTIERLAND

ABOVE: *The 1955 home of Casa de Fritos. From 1957 to 1961, this building was the home of the Silver Banjo Barbecue, operated by actor Don DeFore, one of Walt's good friends. The building is still there today (but hard to recognize) as part of the River Belle Terrace.*

RIGHT: *The Frito Kid, a cleverly disguised vending machine, beckoned guests to drop a nickel in the box—and his friend "Klondike" would "mine" a fresh bag of tasty corn chips just for them.*

BELOW: *In 1955, local Explorer Scouts practiced water rescues off a scrubby atoll in the middle of the Rivers of America, which would, a year later, become Tom Sawyer Island.*

ABOVE: *The Stage Coach station in Frontierland, circa 1959.*

LEFT: *A very rare view of the Miniature Horse Corral seen from the inside, with Frontierland in the background.*

BELOW: *Conestoga Wagons crossing a Frontierland stream, circa 1955.*

Frontier Adventure on
BIG THUNDER

With its earthquakes, spinning opossums, dynamite-chewing goat, and howling coyotes, Big Thunder Mountain Railroad ("the wildest ride in the wilderness") opened on September 15, 1979. Reminiscent of the fanciful red-rock buttes of Bryce Canyon National Park in Utah, the landscape of Big Thunder Mountain Railroad is dotted with authentic and imaginative sights.

Disney Imagineers scouted swap meets, auctions, ghost towns, and abandoned mines throughout the West in order to find the genuine, antique gold-rush-era mining equipment located along the walkway to the Big Thunder Mountain railroad depot, including a 1,200-pound cogwheel used to break down ore, a hand-powered drill press, and a 10-foot-tall, 1880 stamp mill.

The little mining town at the base of Big Thunder Mountain, called Rainbow Ridge, was the original departure point for the former attraction, Mine Train Thru Nature's Wonderland.

ABOVE: The trains of Big Thunder Mountain Railroad come to a "splashing" finale in Dinosaur Gulch.

OPPOSITE: The towering buttes of Big Thunder Mountain Railroad. The engines of the Big Thunder trains sport eyebrow-raising names such as I.M. Brave, U.B. Bold, I.B. Hearty, and I.M. Fearless.

Welcome to
BIG THUNDER

THE BIGGEST
LITTLE BOOM TOWN
IN THE WEST

POP 2,015 2AV 00
ELEVATION 135 FT. 38

What was there before Big Thunder?

NATURE'S WONDERLAND

ABOVE: *A different type of "engineer" is seen working along the railroad tracks of Nature's Wonderland.*

Mine Train Thru Nature's Wonderland opened on May 28, 1960, and featured 204 lifelike inhabitants of such attraction points of interest as Beaver Valley, Bear Country, and The Living Desert (inspired by Walt Disney's *True-Life Adventure* nature documentaries). Guests aboard the Mine Train experienced a very convincing journey into the wilderness, filled with scenic vistas and an abundance of wildlife. Walt Disney himself designed the layout of this fondly remembered attraction.

ABOVE: *The Mine Train annoys a brown bear as he takes his afternoon swim.*

TOP RIGHT: *Beaver Valley.*

RIGHT: *This lake, previously part of the attraction's "Bear Country," can now be seen along the walkway of Big Thunder Trail.*

ABOVE: *The Living Desert section of Nature's Wonderland provided a sun-baked contrast to the surrounding greenery of Frontierland.*

BELOW: *Sharp eyes will spy a mountain lion ready to pounce on its prey and a precariously perched bobcat in this scene from Nature's Wonderland.*

NATURE'S WONDERLAND

LEFT: *Geothermal activity was in abundance in Nature's Wonderland, including the curdling, multicolored muds of the Devil's Paint Pots and the thunderous eruptions of Old "Unfaithful" geyser.*

BELOW: *A panoramic view of The Living Desert portion of Nature's Wonderland.*

So, what was there before Nature's Wonderland?

RAINBOW MOUNTAIN

The distinctive green, black, and steel-blue trains of the Rainbow Mountain Mining & Exploration Company first began transporting would-be miners into the wilderness on July 2, 1956. The Rainbow Caverns Mine Train chugged across a cactus-studded desert on its way to the impressive finale deep inside Rainbow Mountain.

The fluorescent Rainbow Caverns featured 22 breathtaking water effects (including waterfalls, fountains, and geysers), multicolored stalactites and stalagmites, and a choir of otherworldly voices.

ABOVE: *The beautiful fluorescent waterfalls of Rainbow Caverns, designed by Disney Imagineer Claude Coats.*

OPPOSITE: *Guests aboard the Mine Train were startled by teetering rocks and comical cacti. Eagle eyes will notice tiny Native American pueblos atop the mesa in the background.*

Well then, what was there before Rainbow Mountain?

TRAILS!

With imagery that looked more akin to a national park than a theme park, Frontierland was originally crisscrossed with trails for various modes of pioneer transportation, including such Opening Day attractions as the Stage Coach (later dubbed Rainbow Mountain Stage Coaches) and Pack Mules (soon after renamed Rainbow Ridge Pack Mules and Pack Mules Thru Nature's Wonderland). Authentic Conestoga Wagons were also featured from 1955 to 1959.

LEFT: *Guests ride "shotgun" aboard the Stage Coach through very barren badlands.*

BELOW LEFT AND RIGHT: *The Stage Coach gallops through scenery straight out of the American southwest. From these photos it's hard to believe the Pacific Ocean is only 20 minutes away!*

BOTTOM: *A rare color photograph of one of the short-lived Conestoga Wagons traveling along the banks of the Rivers of America.*

FUN

Your day made special—
Disneyland style!

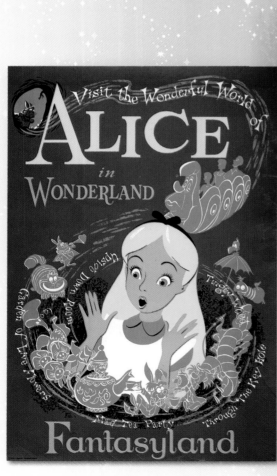

TOM SAWYER ISLAND

EXPLORE!

INJUN JOE'S CAVE, FORT WILDERNESS,
BOTTOMLESS PIT, THE
INDIAN TER...

FRONTIERLAND

FLY YOUR OWN
FLYING SAUCER

space terminal in
TOMORROWLAND

The words "Disneyland" and "fun" are virtually synonymous. When guests enter the Main Gate they are immediately greeted by the grinning, flowering face of Mickey Mouse at the base of the Main Street Train Station—created by more than 50 different varieties of flowers and replanted nine times a year. That familiar icon instantly communicates to each and every guest, regardless of language barriers, that they are in a special place where fun, laughter, and happiness are the order of the day. As guests walk through the tunnels into Town Square, plaques reiterate the message that they have entered a special land of fun: "Here you leave today and enter the world of yesterday, tomorrow, and fantasy."

The Fun of
FANTASYLAND

ABOVE: *The foundation is set for Sleeping Beauty Castle.*

It has been said that of all the different realms of Disneyland, Fantasyland was the one closest to Walt Disney's heart, for it is here that all of Disney's beloved animated films and characters come to life in three dimensions. As guests entered the original Fantasyland, which stood from 1955 to 1982, they walked through Sleeping Beauty Castle and into what appeared to be a lively medieval tournament atmosphere, a colorful landscape filled with candy-striped tents, heraldry banners, flags, and an ample dose of pixie dust.

The early Fantasyland certainly had its charms and appeal, such as Captain Hook's Pirate Ship and Restaurant, Skull Rock Cove, Fantasyland Theater, and the Skyway. However, the overall design of the land, especially the attraction exteriors, consisted of painted flat facades that did not lend themselves to the convincing fairy-tale village Walt and his Imagineers had in mind.

As fond as Walt was of the concept of Fantasyland, he was frustrated by the fact that his finances did not allow him to create the highly detailed and fanciful land he initially envisioned. On May 25, 1983, the New Fantasyland opened, fulfilling Walt's desire for a wholly engrossing experience, complete with highly detailed exteriors, revamped and updated interiors, and the addition of an all-new attraction—Pinocchio's Daring Journey.

TOP: *Finishing touches, such as the turrets, are added to Sleeping Beauty Castle.*

BOTTOM: *Prefabricated spire elements await placement atop the castle battlements.*

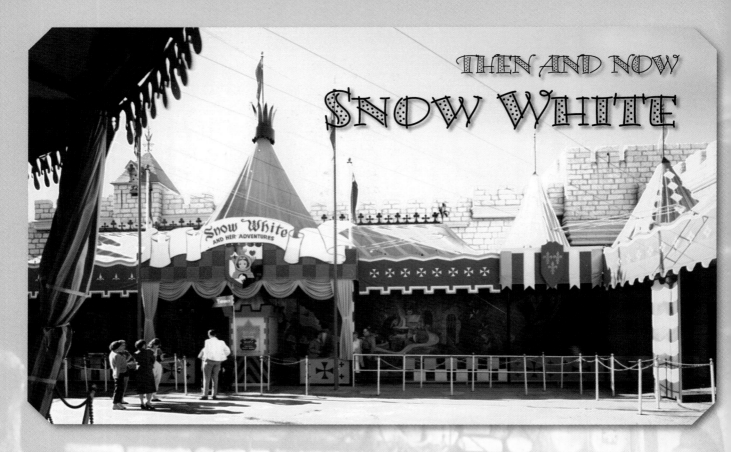

SNOW WHITE

One of the original Fantasyland "dark rides" (so named for their use of ultraviolet black lights and fluorescent set pieces), Snow White's Adventures was one of the most popular of the Fantasyland attractions from 1955 to 1982. A sign at the entrance to the attraction, featuring the Witch, reminded all would-be riders that the attraction was scary. However, such warnings didn't discourage some riders from consistently stealing the Witch's poisoned apple.

With the creation of the New Fantasyland in 1983, Snow White's Adventures was transformed into Snow White's Scary Adventures, receiving a complete makeover of both the exterior and the interior of the attraction. The exterior took its visual cue from the castle of the Evil Queen, complete with an imposing tower from which she can (and does) occasionally stare down on unsuspecting guests. The problem of the ever-missing poisoned apple was solved by new hologram technology.

TOP: *The attraction facade for Snow White's Adventures as seen in 1955.*

ABOVE: *Snow White herself did not appear in her own attraction until 1983.*

ABOVE: *The Seven Dwarfs perform a "Silly Song."*

RIGHT: *The Witch conjures up the infamous poisoned apple.*

BELOW: *The elaborate new entrance to Snow White's Scary Adventures in 1983.*

THEN AND NOW PETER PAN

Peter Pan's Flight is one of the most consistently popular of all the original Fantasyland attractions. Filled with fanciful special effects (including over 175 miles of fiber optics) and memorable scenes from Walt Disney's 1953 animated film *Peter Pan*, the attraction was completely refurbished in 1983 and re-opened with an all-new exterior and exciting new effects and scenes. Sharp-eyed guests will notice the unique weathervane atop the exterior clock tower (in the shape of Captain Hook's galleon) and passersby can frequently hear the Darling children (Wendy, Michael, and John) playing in the nursery.

OPPOSITE TOP: *The original 1955 exterior facade of Peter Pan's Flight.*

OPPOSITE MIDDLE: *Flying over Never Land inside the redesigned Peter Pan's Flight.*

TOP LEFT: *Concept sketch for Captain Hook's galleon.*

LEFT: *The exterior of Peter Pan's Flight, featuring its impressive clock tower and Matterhorn Mountain backdrop.*

THEN AND NOW
MR. TOAD

Mr. Toad's Wild Ride, based on the 1949 Disney animated feature *The Adventures of Ichabod and Mr. Toad*, is one of the three original Fantasyland dark rides. Since its debut in 1955, it has been a favorite with young, would-be drivers who can't resist an attraction where the rules of the road are of no concern.

Completely redesigned in 1983, the madcap adventure now resembles stately Toad Hall, where the eccentric Mr. Toad himself takes everyone on a wild ride across the English countryside. Along the way, drivers race and crash through Mr. Toad's wacky adventures. The attraction requires numerous visits to catch all of its in-jokes and sight gags, such as the insignia on Toad's coat of arms ("Toadi Acceleratio Semper Absurda"—translation: "Speeding with Toad is always absurd") and the book titles in the library (*Frogean Psychology*, *A Tadpole Grows in Brooklyn*, and *For Whom the Toads Croak*).

OPPOSITE TOP: *Mr. Toad's Wild Ride in 1955.*

LEFT: *Concept sketch of Toad Hall interior by Disney artist Claude Coats.*

TOP: *Toad Hall in Fantasyland today.*

ABOVE: *Tunnel 13 from the original 1955 version of Mr. Toad's Wild Ride.*

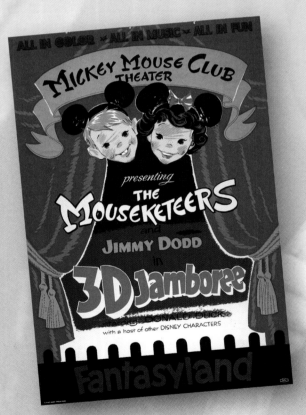

The Mickey Mouse Club Theater opened on August 27, 1955, featuring a program of Disney cartoon shorts and was the official Disneyland headquarters for the Mouseketeers until 1963. On June 16, 1956, the theater debuted a program featuring a state-of-the-art 3-D film called *3D Jamboree* (starring the Mouseketeers), plus the 3-D Donald Duck cartoon *Working for Peanuts*, and the first 3-D cartoon ever produced, *Adventures in Music: Melody*.

In 1964 the theater was renamed the Fantasyland Theater. Pinocchio's Daring Journey, based on Walt Disney's classic animated feature *Pinocchio*, replaced the Fantasyland Theater in 1983. The exterior features such Tyrolean motifs as gabled rooftops, cobblestone pathways, Stromboli's marionette show over the entrance, and a prominent Monstro the Whale weathervane. Perhaps the most atmospheric of all the Fantasyland dark rides, Pinocchio's Daring Journey accurately brings to life all the old-world charm and whimsy of the beloved film.

TOP: *The Mickey Mouse Club Theater as it appeared from 1955 to 1964.*

ABOVE: *A Disneyland attraction poster for* 3D Jamboree, *starring the original Mouseketeers.*

TOP LEFT: *Geppetto, Pinocchio, and little Figaro celebrate a wish come true.*

TOP RIGHT: *The villainous Foulfellow and Gideon find time for play on Pleasure Island.*

ABOVE: *The charming entrance to Pinocchio's Daring Journey as it is today.*

Fun with
CAPTAIN HOOK

Inspired by Walt Disney's popular 1953 animated film version of *Peter Pan*, Captain Hook's Pirate Ship (seen above) was a Fantasyland landmark from 1955 to 1982, standing on the site where Dumbo flies today. The ship was both an interactive playground for little would-be scalawags and a restaurant. Guests went below decks to the "galley" to order appropriately-themed seafood items, consisting mainly of tuna specialties. From the uppermost deck of the ship, near the helm, guests received a spectacular panoramic view of Fantasyland down below.

In 1960 Skull Rock Cove was added to the lagoon where Captain Hook's Pirate Ship was moored. The new addition was primarily a tropical canopied dining area that provided a shady and quiet respite from the whimsy of Fantasyland. Directly adjacent to the dining area was the imposing visage of Skull Rock itself with its mysterious caverns, crevices, and thundering waterfalls. In the evening Skull Rock became even more ominous as the "eyes" in the rock glowed with a haunting green luminescence.

ABOVE: *Peter Pan stood guard over Skull Rock Cove in Fantasyland in the 1970s.*

LEFT: *Diners enjoyed a cool, shady oasis under the watchful eye of the skull.*

Storytelling Fun in STORYBOOK LAND

In the midst of all the bustling whimsy of Fantasyland is the Storybook Land Canal Boats attraction, which opened on June 16, 1956. Guests begin their tranquil voyage by being swallowed by Monstro the Whale and then pass miniature scenes from some of Disney's most beloved animated features, including Geppetto's Village, the forest of the Seven Dwarfs, Toad Hall, Aladdin's city of Agrabah, and the seaside palace of Prince Eric from *The Little Mermaid*, plus Cinderella Castle (the tallest structure and highest point in Storybook Land). Created at 1/12th scale, the intricately detailed dwellings are complemented by actual living miniature shrubs, flowers, and trees, including 155-year-old miniature pine trees. Each of the Storybook Land Canal Boats has been christened with an appropriate name, such as Snow White, Aurora, Cinderella, Alice, Faline, Wendy, and Tinker Bell.

LEFT: *Cinderella Castle is one of the visual "high points" in Storybook Land.*

BOTTOM: *The windmills below were inspired by Walt Disney's cartoon short "The Old Mill" (1937).*

LEFT: *Toad Hall, the ancestral home of J. Thaddeus Toad, is just one of many famous miniature homes to be found along the shores of the Storybook Land canals.*

What was there before Storybook Land?

LEFT: *The Canal Boats of the World was the forerunner of today's Storybook Land. The attraction was euphemistically referred to as "Mud Banks of the World" because there was initially virtually nothing to see! The attraction premiered on July 17, 1955 and was renamed Storybook Land on September 16, 1955, with the arrival of the miniature scenes we know today.*

Fun with THE FUTURE

TOP: *Walt Disney peers into the future, and a brand-new monorail cabin, circa 1959.*

TOP RIGHT: America the Beautiful *in Tomorrowland, the second in a series of 360-degree circular films, following the original Circarama which opened in July 1955.* America the Beautiful *actually premiered at the Brussels World's Fair in 1958 and was transformed into an attraction for Disneyland in 1960. The film was updated in 1967 and 1975, then replaced in 1984 by* American Journeys.

RIGHT: *From 1956 to 1963 multihued wonders, displays, and paint swatches filled The Color Gallery in Tomorrowland.*

TOP: Who knew aluminum could be so fun? Guests of the Hall of Aluminum Fame in Tomorrowland did. The future seemed bright and very shiny with all of the (then) new aluminum products on display.

TOP RIGHT: Kap, the Aluminum Pig, wearing a pair of overalls and holding a ready wrench, was the mascot of the Hall of Aluminum Fame. The pig refers to the term "Pig aluminum," the unrefined, rough form of the metal.

RIGHT: The Dairy Bar was featured in Tomorrowland from 1956 to 1958. Here guests could learn all about farming techniques of the future, including the prospect of flying milkmen delivering milk straight to the front door and how happy cows produce better milk. After the lesson, guests could enjoy an ice-cold glass of milk at the bar.

Fun with Plastic

TOP: *The House of the Future, gift–wrapped for the holidays.*

LEFT AND BELOW: *The House of the Future featured modern rooms for adults and children, and a comfy, plastic den for everyone.*

The House of the Future, located to the left of the entrance to Tomorrowland, was a modernistic, four-winged, cantilevered display home where guests could see the very latest gadgets and gizmos for the most modern of homes, circa 1957–1967. Constructed entirely of plastic, the house had a recorded narration informing the guests that "hardly a natural material appears anywhere in the house." When it was time to demolish it, the wrecking ball simply bounced off the plastic, necessitating that the entire House be taken apart by hand, saw, and crowbar, piece by plastic piece.

The Hall of Chemistry stood at the entrance to Tomorrowland where today's Star Tours attraction is located. Through animated displays and oversized props, the attraction provided an overview of how chemicals contribute to modern living. The Hall of Chemistry was a landmark from 1955 until it evaporated from the Tomorrowland landscape in September 1966.

Premiering on August 16, 1955, the Phantom Boats of Tomorrowland have the dubious distinction of being the first attraction ever removed from Disneyland. Although their retro design, featuring large "space age"-inspired tail fins, was appealing, their high operating costs and constant maintenance problems were not. The attraction quickly faded into memory by the fall of 1956.

The Fun of CRITTER COUNTRY

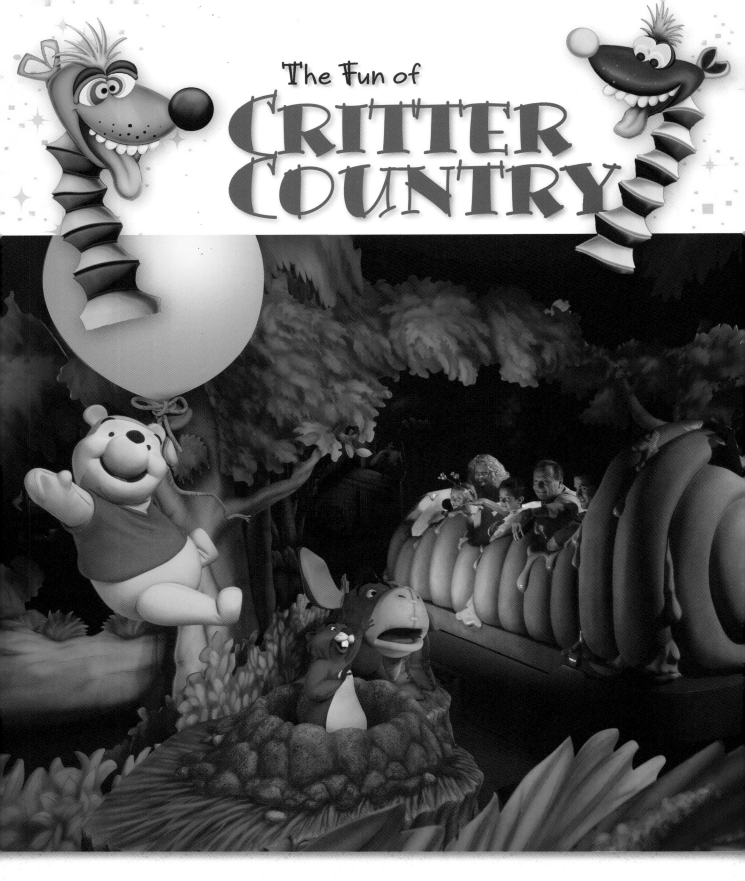

ABOVE: *A "Beehicle" filled with delighted guests greets Gopher, Eeyore, and Winnie the Pooh.*

On November 23, 1988, a new land was introduced at Disneyland—Critter Country. This little backwoods oasis is a world unto its own, with shady trees and cool streams, the perfect woodland home for all kinds of cuddly and furry inhabitants. Critter Country is home to both Splash Mountain and The Many Adventures of Winnie the Pooh.

As the newest addition to Critter Country, The Many Adventures of Winnie the Pooh brings to life the delightful tales of the "bear with very little brain" and all of his friends from the Hundred Acre Wood. Based on Walt Disney's beloved animated featurettes *Winnie the Pooh and the Honey Tree* (1966) and *Winnie the Pooh and the Blustery Day* (1968), the new attraction was designed to fit perfectly within the building that formerly housed the Country Bear Jamboree.

To begin their adventures with Pooh and his friends, guests board one of 22 "beehicles" outside of the attraction in an environment that evokes a real-life Hundred Acre Wood, with calming streams and high birch and evergreen elms, plus Eeyore's stick house, Rabbit's garden, and numerous visuals of dripping honey.

Inside the attraction guests go on a journey with Pooh as he experiences a rather "Blustery Day," encounters a very energetic Tigger, and has a nightmare of honey-stealing Huffalumps and Woozles, all ending with a "Hip, Hip Pooh-ray" party. The adventure is accompanied by the familiar musical score from the Winnie the Pooh featurettes, and was incorporated into the attraction under the supervision of Disney Legends Richard M. Sherman and Buddy Baker. Richard, along with his brother Robert B. Sherman, wrote the songs and Buddy conducted and arranged the score for the original "Pooh" featurettes.

TOP: *Winnie the Pooh is the guest of honor at a celebration in the finale of The Many Adventures of Winnie the Pooh.*

ABOVE: *Pooh enjoys a large "smackerel" of honey.*

What was there before Critter Country?
BEAR COUNTRY

Bear Country became a part of the Disneyland landscape in 1972. Re-creating the look and feel of the American northwest of the late 1800s, this wilderness outpost was just a short walk away from the jazz and adventures of New Orleans Square. Guests entered the new "land" by passing the cliff-side cave of the very loudly snoring Rufus the bear. The signature attraction of Bear Country was the Country Bear Jamboree, a mirthful salute to America's country-western musical heritage presented by a playhouse full of talented bruins. Other points of interest included the Mile Long Bar (inside, it really did *look* a mile long), Teddi Barra's Swingin' Arcade (named for the chanteuse of the Country Bear Jamboree), Ursus H. Bear's Wilderness Outpost, Explorer Canoes down on the river, and for those with a growling stomach, the Hungry Bear Restaurant.

TOP: *Guests look over the construction fence to view progress on Bear Country.*

ABOVE: *Bear Country under construction in the early 1970s. The large wood structure on the left would soon be the home of the Country Bear Jamboree.*

Well then, what was there before Bear Country?
INDIAN VILLAGE

The Indian Village was a part of Frontierland from 1955 to 1971. Located in the same area as present-day Critter Country, the Indian Village featured an amalgam of Native American dwellings and customs, from totem poles to birch bark lodges to the teepees of the Plains Indians. Native American performers presented traditional dances and demonstrations of bow-and-arrow technique. The Indian Village had a starring role in the 1970 "Disneyland Showtime" episode of Disney's popular Sunday night TV series, *The Wonderful World of Disney*.

TOP, LEFT TO RIGHT: *Authentic teepees, totem poles and birch bark lodges.*

ABOVE: *The wilderness of Frontierland, circa 1955. Fowler's Harbor (center) still stands today, but now Splash Mountain towers to the left and Tom Sawyer Island is to the right.*

OPPOSITE: *Archery demonstrations at the Indian Village, along the Rivers of America. Note the real dirt walkways that could be found throughout Frontierland in the early days.*

THRILLS

Hang onto your hats!

For baby boomers who grew up with Disneyland, nothing elicited a thrill like the sight of Matterhorn Mountain rising over the Park's earthen berm, signaling to all guests arriving by car that they had arrived at "The Happiest Place on Earth." For today's generation, the thrill and anticipation is the same, but the icons have expanded to include not only the snowy slopes of the Matterhorn, but also Big Thunder Mountain, Space Mountain, and Splash Mountain. The psychological appeal of being excited and thrilled is an integral part of the Disneyland experience, and to satisfy eager thrill-seekers Disneyland continues to provide world-class excitement with state-of-the-art fun.

SPACE STATION X-1

Look into the future. See America from *OUTER SPACE*

TOMORROWLAND

The Thrills of
SPACE MOUNTAIN

Space Mountain was officially introduced as part of Tomorrowland on May 4, 1977, during Opening Day festivities attended by the original U.S. Mercury Astronauts (America's first men in space). The immensely popular attraction can trace its lineage back to a concept Walt Disney had in the early 1960s for a "Space Port and Rocket Flight" type of adventure. Overall, Space Mountain was 12 years in the making, with over one million man-hours utilized in design and construction.

Space Mountain rises 118 feet into the Tomorrowland skyline, while the foundation extends 20 feet into the ground, containing an impressive 3,500 feet of track under its unique and recognizable spires. The familiar brilliant white exterior of the mountain was temporarily changed in 1998 to reflect the gold and bronze colors of the New Tomorrowland but was changed back to its traditional gleaming white in 2004. A wholly re-Imagineered Space Mountain was created to celebrate the 50th anniversary of Disneyland in 2005.

ABOVE: *The original Space Mountain complex that opened in 1977 included the world-famous Space Stage, as well as the Space Place restaurant and the Starcade arcade.*

RIGHT: *The rarely seen interior track is a maze of tightly intertwined twists and turns.*

RIGHT: *The gold and bronze patina of Space Mountain, 1998.*

BELOW: *Newly designed rockets soar through an all-new Space Mountain, introduced as part of the 50th Anniversary celebration.*

What was there before Space Mountain?

ABOVE: *The Tomorrowland Stage, located adjacent to Flight to the Moon, played host to various big-name acts from 1967 until 1977. The fondly remembered "Kids of the Kingdom" singing group were frequent performers, along with appearances by the Disney Characters. On July 20, 1969, the Tomorrowland Stage was filled to capacity as guests stood shoulder-to-shoulder, watching a live broadcast of the historic moon landing of Apollo 11.*

LEFT: *From 1961 to 1966 Flying Saucers could be seen "hovering" over Tomorrowland, literally floating just inches off the ground atop a column of air in this fondly remembered attraction. In a unique futuristic twist on the classic "bumper cars" of the past, passengers tilted their bodies forward or backward in order to "fly" the saucer across the arena (think of a life-size air hockey game). The Flying Saucers were replaced by the Tomorrowland Stage in 1967, and today Space Mountain stands on their former site.*

ABOVE LEFT: *Walt Disney rides a prototype of the Flying Saucers, seeming none too pleased by the consistent mechanical problems that would eventually lead to the attraction's demise.*

ABOVE RIGHT: *Guests await their turn to "hover on air" on the Flying Saucers.*

The Thrills of
THE MATTERHORN

The Matterhorn Bobsleds opened in Fantasyland on June 14, 1959, and is noteworthy for many "firsts"—first thrill attraction created for Disneyland, first tubular steel roller-coaster ever built, first fully themed indoor/outdoor coaster, and the first roller-coaster that allowed multiple vehicles on the same track at once.

The Matterhorn is unique to Disneyland—it has never been replicated at any of the other Disney theme parks around the world.

The famous attraction was inspired by Walt Disney's interest in Switzerland (site of one of his family vacations) and his 1959 live-action film *Third Man on the Mountain*, a story of mountain climbers of the famous peak near Zermatt, Switzerland.

The mighty Matterhorn, a 1/100th replica of its Swiss namesake, is the tallest structure inside Disneyland, towering 147 feet over the Park. To create the mountain, Disney Imagineers used enough lumber to build twenty-seven 1950s-era tract homes, 2,175 individual steel girders, and countless tons of concrete. The movie industry technique of forced perspective was used to make the mountain appear larger than it actually is, utilizing progressively smaller trees and landscaping that give the illusion of more height as your eye travels upward.

OPPOSITE: *The buckets of the Skyway passed through the center of the Matterhorn until 1994.*

TOP LEFT AND RIGHT: *The original single-car bobsled, and the two-car bobsled introduced in 1978.*

BACKGROUND: *The Abominable Snowman lies in wait to surprise unsuspecting mountaineers.*

What was there before the Matterhorn?

Once upon a time at Disneyland there was a scrubby, grass-covered mound of earth called Holiday Hill. This little patch of dirt served as both the dividing line between Fantasyland and Tomorrowland and home to the very unattractive center steel tower that supported the Skyway attraction. Following a visit to Switzerland, Walt Disney became fascinated with the idea of creating a toboggan attraction for Holiday Hill. In anticipation of this possible new adventure, the official name of Holiday Hill was changed to Snow Hill in early 1956. Snow Hill never saw any flurries but it did see its share of stolen kisses, eventually becoming the Disneyland version of a 1950s drive-in backseat.

In 1959, the little mound of dirt became the home of the famous Matterhorn Bobsleds.

RIGHT: *Exploring the pathways of Holiday Hill.*

OPPOSITE: *Once Holiday Hill, a view of the future location of the Matterhorn, seen from Main Street.*

RIGHT: *The steel skeleton of the Matterhorn rises on the former site of Holiday Hill, in 1958.*

BELOW: *A rare aerial view of Holiday Hill in 1955, before the addition of the Skyway tower.*

BOTTOM: *The visually inappropriate center tower of the Skyway stood atop Holiday Hill in 1956, towering over Storybook Land below. The location of that tower, at the midpoint of the Skyway cables, provided Disney's Imagineers with the exact position and height for Matterhorn Mountain's framework.*

The Thrills of
INDIANA JONES™

In March, 1995, the Indiana Jones™ Adventure was uncovered and opened in the dense jungle of Adventureland. One of the most complex Disney theme park attractions ever created, the Indiana Jones™ Adventure brings to life the exploits of the noted archaeologist and adventurer, initially made famous in the 1982 film *Raiders of the Lost Ark*.

Set in 1935, the breathtaking attraction takes guests on a hair-raising quest through the Temple of the Forbidden Eye in search of hidden treasures, eternal youth, and visions of the future. An unfortunate encounter with Mara, the temple deity, results in a series of escapes from her evil clutches, including encounters with snakes (*Why did it have to be snakes?*), bats, fire, booby traps, a collapsing bamboo bridge, thousands of rats, and a 5-ton rampaging boulder.

Intrepid explorers journey through the attraction on one of sixteen unique troop-transport vehicles. Each vehicle features its very own onboard computer system that monitors all aspects of the attraction, including audio, lighting, and course—the system is capable of 160,000 unique journey combinations.

ABOVE: *The Indiana Jones™ Adventure is one of the most technically sophisticated and detailed Disney theme park attractions in the world.*

RIGHT: *"Tourists . . . why did it have to be tourists?"*

OPPOSITE: *The Indiana Jones™ Adventure provides Disneyland guests with unforgettable thrills.*

Thrills in
OUTER SPACE

Man's desire to fly, soar, and discover has been a characteristic defining Tomorrowland over the past five decades. Through the years, countless guests have experienced "lift-off" in attractions that have allowed them to sail over America, visit the Moon of Endor, explore the Moon and Mars of our own solar system, race through the darkness of space, or chart their own flight pattern over Tomorrowland itself.

These attractions have not only delivered thrills in the air but they have also become a part of Disneyland's rich aviation history.

OPPOSITE: *Originally known as Space Station X-1, Satellite-View of America provided guests with an incredible view of North America as seen from an orbiting satellite. The attraction orbited Tomorrowland from 1956 to 1960.*

CENTER: *Guests flew almost 70 feet off the ground during their exciting voyage aboard the Rocket Jets, featured in Tomorrowland from 1967 to 1998.*

BACKGROUND: *Astro Orbitor is the current incarnation of the Rocket Jets.*

BELOW: *Guests piloted their own Astro-Jets in Tomorrowland from 1956 to 1964, when the attraction's name was changed to Tomorrowland Jets.*

BOTTOM: *The Court of Honor featured 48 state flags showcased within an eight-pointed, star-shaped planter in Tomorrowland. In 1956, this site welcomed the Astro-Jets. The flagpoles were relocated, and for the decade from 1956 to 1966, they graced the entrance to Tomorrowland.*

MUSIC

You'd notice it if it wasn't there

"it's a small world"

JOIN THE HAPPIEST CRUISE THAT EVER SAILED 'ROUND THE WORLD

PRESENTED BY **BANK OF AMERICA**

Fantasyland

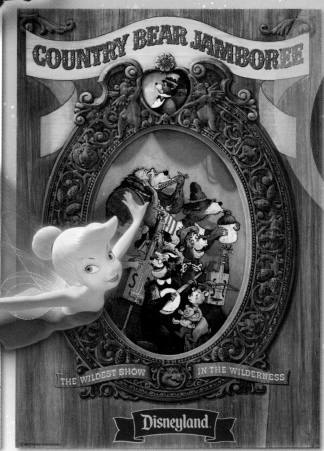

COUNTRY BEAR JAMBOREE

THE WILDEST SHOW   IN THE WILDERNESS

Disneyland.

Music is as much a part of the magic of Disneyland as Mickey Mouse, Tinker Bell, and Sleeping Beauty Castle. Over the last five decades, Disneyland has introduced many memorable and beloved songs. Additionally, Disneyland has helped to introduce children to the wonders of live music and performance, inspiring more than a few of today's top entertainers. From the simple rinky-tink sound of a ragtime piano on Main Street, U.S.A., to orchestrated stage musicals, music has made an indelible imprint on the ears of every guest who has ever entered "The Happiest Place on Earth."

The Music of
"IT'S A SMALL WORLD"

Walt Disney unveiled "it's a small world" at Disneyland on May 28, 1966, following its successful inaugural run at the 1964–1965 New York World's Fair. One of the most beloved Disney theme park attractions of all time, "it's a small world" is a fun-filled and whimsical salute to the children of the world that conveys its message of peace and harmony through the international language of music.

Richard M. Sherman and Robert B. Sherman, the prolific songwriting team behind such Disney film classics as *Mary Poppins, The Jungle Book,* and *The Many Adventures of Winnie the Pooh*, penned the world-famous title song at the personal request of Walt Disney. The attraction was originally supposed to feature a medley of national anthems from the countries represented in the boat journey. However, the result was a cacophony of noise. Instead, the Sherman Brothers' catchy roundelay proved to convey perfectly the spirit and childlike wonder of the attraction.

Although the song, officially entitled "It's A Small World (After All)," premiered at the World's Fair in 1964, it was the Disneyland attraction that popularized it beyond expectations. Today, the theme is one of the most performed and recognized songs the world over.

On November 27, 1997, a new twist on "it's a small world" was introduced, called "it's a small world" holiday. This all-new festive winter overlay highlights the holidays as celebrated around the world, with the attraction's memorable theme song cleverly intertwined with two holiday classics, "Deck the Halls" and "Jingle Bells."

BACKGROUND: *The impressive façade of "it's a small world" features iconic world landmarks, a glockenspiel clock, and 22-karat gold leafing on its spire and finials.*

TOP RIGHT AND MIDDLE: *"it's a small world" holiday adds a festive overlay to the exterior and interior of the world-famous attraction.*

BELOW LEFT TO RIGHT: *The children of the world, as represented in "it's a small world."*

The Madcap Musical Adventures of
ALICE IN WONDERLAND

The Academy Award–nominated film score to Walt Disney's 1951 classic animated film *Alice in Wonderland* forms the basis for this wacky and enchanting Fantasyland attraction. Three years following the opening of Disneyland, Walt created an attraction version of his delightful film as a complement to the spinning and popular Mad Tea Party attraction. The original incarnation of Alice in Wonderland included visits to the Upside Down Room, a garden of oversized flowers, and the court of the Queen of Hearts.

In April of 1984 a completely remodeled and expanded version of the attraction opened, still featuring the comical vehicles modeled after the film's snobbish Caterpillar. However, the new version of Alice in Wonderland put much more emphasis on modern-day special effects, plus the film's music and corresponding scenes, including songs such as "I'm Late," "The Unbirthday Song," "March of the Cards," and "Painting the Roses Red." For the sake of authenticity, Kathryn Beaumont, the original speaking and singing voice of Alice from the film, also provided Alice's vocals for the 1984 remake of the attraction.

ABOVE: *The White Rabbit finds out he's late for a very important date.*

BACKGROUND: *The Mad Hatter and March Hare enjoy a spot of tea during their Very Merry Unbirthday party.*

RIGHT: *Original concept art by Disney Legend Mary Blair. The Alice in Wonderland attraction opened in 1958.*

BOTTOM: *A cutaway rendering of the original attraction's scenes.*

The Music of THE HAUNTED MANSION

OPPOSITE AND INSET TOP: *The organ base in the ballroom of The Haunted Mansion once belonged to the infamous Captain Nemo—it is the original organ prop from Walt Disney's 1954 live-action film 20,000 Leagues Under the Sea.*

TOP RIGHT AND MIDDLE: *In Haunted Mansion Holiday, Jack Skellington (as "Sandy Claws") welcomes the "foolish mortals" to a celebration they won't soon forget.*

BOTTOM RIGHT AND OPPOSITE INSET LEFT: *Ghostly bands of musicians provide musical accompaniment to the tune of "Grim Grinning Ghosts" in the graveyard of The Haunted Mansion.*

Like great films, Disneyland attractions often have memorable music that through the years has become classic with age—so familiar, so beloved that it is instantly recognizable and immediately evokes the mood and the feel of the attraction. Such is the case with The Haunted Mansion.

The main theme of the attraction is the song "Grim Grinning Ghosts," written by Disney Imagineer X Atencio and famed Disney music composer, arranger, and conductor Buddy Baker. This single piece of music is the audio thread that links each portion of the attraction and sets the tone of each scene—the song is heard at various times as a funeral dirge, a waltz, and a zany ragtime-like tune. The soundtrack to The Haunted Mansion, based on this one song, is as popular as any blockbuster Hollywood film, past or present.

In October 2001, The Haunted Mansion received a startling transformation into Haunted Mansion Holiday. The now seasonal makeover showcases the tale of Jack Skellington, the pumpkin king of Halloweentown from the classic stop-motion animated film *Tim Burton's The Nightmare Before Christmas*, as he tries to take over the holidays in the guise of "Sandy Claws," resulting in a fantastic collision of holiday spirits.

The Music of THE GOLDEN HORSESHOE

On July 17, 1955, the very first Disney-produced stage show, the Golden Horseshoe Revue, officially premiered inside Slue Foot Sue's Golden Horseshoe saloon in Frontierland. This rollicking Wild West revue soon became one of the most popular attractions at the Park, playing to packed houses several times a day. Walt Disney personally auditioned and selected the inaugural cast of the show, and was a frequent audience member.

The program starred the flirtatious Slue Foot Sue (the owner and proprietor of the saloon), a beguiling Irish tenor, a bevy of can-can dancers, a small pit band, and an eccentric traveling salesman. Audiences were entertained by the music and songs of a bygone era including songs by Stephen Foster, jaunty Irish tunes, Western favorites, and naturally, Offenbach's can-can.

During its 31-year run, the Golden Horseshoe Revue became a favorite stop for visiting celebrities and dignitaries, who usually enjoyed the music and humor-filled show from Walt Disney's private opera box on stage left. Proving the show business maxim that "The show must go on," the various casts of the Golden Horseshoe Revue logged well over 50,000 performances, making it the longest-running stage show in history (according to the *Guinness Book of World Records*) upon its closing on October 12, 1986. Today, the Golden Horseshoe Revue is still one of the most fondly remembered (and requested) attractions from the past.

ABOVE: *A 1956 cast photo featuring stars (left to right) Wally Boag, Betty Taylor, and Donald Novis.*

BELOW LEFT: *No Wild West revue would be complete without a line of beautiful can-can dancers.*

BELOW RIGHT: *From 1962 through 1986, Fulton Burley joined Wally and Betty to play the role of the comical and melodious Irish tenor.*

OPPOSITE LEFT: *Comedian Wally Boag originated the roles of the Traveling Salesman and Pecos Bill, the teeth-spitting, "toughest" critter west of the Alamo.*

OPPOSITE: *The gleaming exterior of the Golden Horseshoe saloon, during the heyday of Slue Foot Sue.*

The Music of
THE COUNTRY BEAR JAMBOREE

Originally envisioned in the mid-1960s by Walt Disney as an entertainment concept for a proposed Disney ski resort in California, the Country Bear Jamboree eventually became a reality as one of the Opening Day Frontierland attractions at Walt Disney World Resort in Florida in October, 1971. Six months later, on March 24, 1972, the Country Bear Jamboree premiered as the signature attraction of Bear Country, an all-new land at Disneyland—the first attraction export to California from Florida.

The "mirthful, musical jamboree" starred 18 Audio-Animatronics performers, including the paw-tapping 5 Bear Rugs, the swingin' Teddi Barra, and the plodding Big Al, in a loving and humorous salute to America's country-western musical legacy. The original show inspired two spin-offs, the Country Bear Christmas Special (premiering November, 1984) and The Country Bear Vacation Hoedown (premiering February, 1986).

After thirty years of foot-stomping performances, the curtains lowered for the last time at the Country Bear Jamboree on September 9, 2001.

OPPOSITE TOP: *Big Al gives a soulful rendition of "Blood on the Saddle."*

OPPOSITE BOTTOM: *The cast gathers for the grand finale.*

ABOVE: *The house band of Grizzly Hall, the 5 Bear Rugs.*

LEFT AND BELOW: *Some of the performers who graced the stage of the Playhouse include (counter–clockwise from top) Wendell, Trixie, Teddi Barra, Gomer, The Sun Bonnets (Bunny, Bubbles, and Beulah), Terrence, and Ernest.*

Our Musical Heritage
AMERICA ON PARADE

Conceived as a musical salute and celebration honoring the American Bicentennial, America on Parade began its daily performances in July 1975, at both Disneyland and Walt Disney World Resort in Florida, and continued until September 1976. In all, the red, white, and blue three-quarter-mile-long parade spectacular's cast of more than 150 performers completed more than 1,200 performances before a total audience of 25 million guests.

"The Great American Band Organ" formed the basis of the soundtrack for "America on Parade," featuring favorite American tunes such as "Yankee Doodle," "O Susannah," "In the Good Old Summertime," and "Stars and Stripes Forever." The "Sadie Mae," a completely restored 1890 automatic band organ, provided the base melodies for the parade with synthesized effects superimposed over the songs to give the parade a festive and unique sound.

ABOVE LEFT: *Mickey, Donald, and Goofy as The Spirit of '76 lead off America on Parade.*

ABOVE RIGHT: *The parade's unique "People of America" characters comprise a traditional fife & drum corps.*

THIS PAGE, CLOCKWISE: *America's heritage parades down Main Street in the form of the Liberty Bell, Betsy Ross, and a musical production number, "Waiting for the Robert E. Lee."*

Ladies and gentlemen, boys and girls, Disneyland proudly presents our spect sparkling lights and electro-syntho-magnetic musical sounds...

THE MAIN STREET ELECTRICAL PARADE

With that announcement the lights on Main Street would dim and the electricity and excitement in the air would double as the wondrous sight of The Main Street Electrical Parade began its procession, illuminating the night sky with enchantment, and delighting guests of all ages.

Making its world premiere at Disneyland on June 17, 1972, The Main Street Electrical Parade has become a tradition at Disney parks around the world. Its depiction of classic Disney film scenes, re-created in over a half million sparkling lights and over 500 miles of wiring, entertained an estimated 75 million guests (the largest audience ever to view a live performance) during its 3,500 trips down Main Street. The parade's 24-year run at Disneyland came to an end in 1996, though it has made special appearances around the world in the years since.

Recognizable almost instantaneously as the parade's main theme is a 1967 composition entitled "Baroque Hoedown," which was cleverly intertwined with classic Disney songs to produce a delightful musical soundtrack. The unique sound of the parade was created utilizing an electronic Moog synthesizer, which gave both the parade and its familiar introduction a distinct sound. The Main Street Electrical Parade was indeed a unique experience of sight and sound.

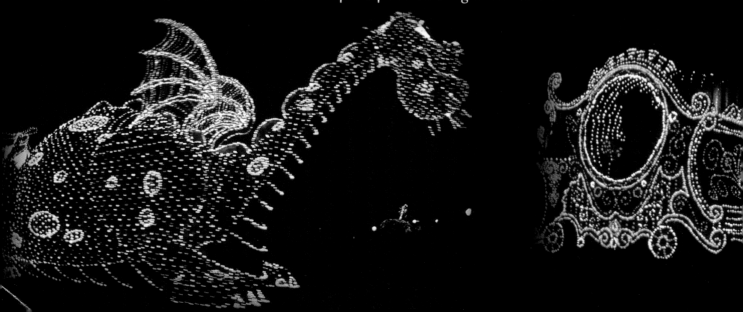

ar festival pageant of nighttime magic and imagination, in thousands of

The Musical Adventures of
Splash Mountain

Disneyland guests can find a "mighty satisfactual" musical experience in the form of Splash Mountain. Inspired by Walt Disney's classic film *Song of the South* and the wise fables of Uncle Remus, Splash Mountain is an exciting and tune-filled flume adventure where guests experience a hair-raising 52-foot, 46-degree-angle, 40-mph plunge into a "Zip-a-Dee-Doo-Dah" finale.

ABOVE: *From the top of Chickapin Hill on Splash Mountain guests plunge down one of the world's longest and steepest flume drops straight into a thorny briar patch below. As the little logs race through the underground cavern at the bottom of the the hill, they become the fastest ride in Disneyland.*

RIGHT: *Brer Bear finds his "Laughing Place" and sticks his nose right into a hive full of bees.*

BELOW: *Brer Rabbit vows to leave his briar patch home for good, headin' for a little more adventure.*

BOTTOM: *Anyone recognize these critters? They used to live in Tomorrowland, and were known for their patriotic singing abilities.*

Music, Music
EVERYWHERE!

No matter where guests turn, Disneyland is simply bursting with melodies and familiar tunes in the form of the variety of musical performances on display throughout the park. From the crowd that routinely gathers around the Coke Corner pianist in the evening to hear toe-tapping ragtime, to the grandeur of the musical spectaculars of the Fantasyland Theater, guests are consistently entertained by the joy of live performance.

Live music and performance has been a tradition at Disneyland since the Disneyland Band first entertained guests on Opening Day. Over the years, some of the biggest names in music have performed at the park while the Disneyland College Marching Band and Magic Music Days program have helped to hone the skills and capabilities of aspiring musicians, singers, and performers.

RIGHT: *The 1956 queue line for the World Beneath Us attraction in Tomorrowland showcased an early attempt to add atmospheric music to the queue by playing John Philip Sousa marches!*

BELOW LEFT: *The Dapper Dans barbershop quartet has been a fixture on Main Street since 1957, and is consistently one of the most popular musical groups in the park.*

BELOW RIGHT: *The Saxophone Quartet on Main Street, U.S.A.*

BELOW: *Snow White—An Enchanting New Musical is the most elaborate stage production ever produced at Disneyland, created as a piece of theater for families with younger children by extraordinary talents who have made their reputations both on Broadway and in the theater.*

ABOVE: *Videopolis, a high-tech teen dance area featuring a 5,000-square-foot dance floor and over 70 video monitors, opened on June 22, 1985. Eleven years later, Videopolis was reborn as the Fantasyland Theater, ushering in a new era of elaborate stage productions.*

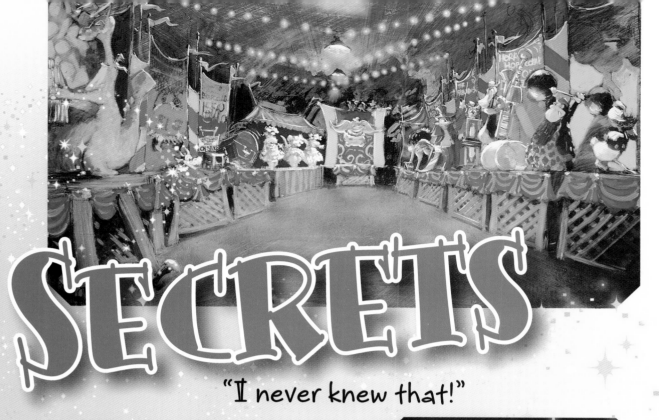

SECRETS

"I never knew that!"

For years inquisitive guests have pondered the many wonders of Disneyland, often resulting in an astonishing exclamation of "How did they do that?!" Every day guests to Disneyland experience hidden secrets that they don't even realize they are experiencing. Sometimes guests get so wrapped up in the atmosphere of a locale or attraction that they fail to notice the minutiae of detail and the captivating back stories that make Disneyland a treasure trove of secrets and trivia. But, like a classically trained magician, Disneyland will never give up all of its secrets.

The Secrets of
AUDIO-ANIMATRONICS

The amazing three-dimensional animation process known as Audio-Animatronics has captivated Disneyland guests for over four decades. "It's sound and animation through electronics," Walt Disney once explained. "We can program whole shows on tape . . . The tape sends signals and the little figures go to work and they sing and act and move according to the impulse that comes from the tape."

On June 23, 1963, Walt and his Imagineers unveiled Walt Disney's Enchanted Tiki Room in Adventureland at Disneyland, considered the very first Audio-Animatronics attraction. When The Enchanted Tiki Room opened, its cast of 225 "AA" figures astounded capacity audiences and received rave reviews.

Almost immediately, Walt was on his way to advancing the technology in the form of four Audio-Animatronics shows he produced for the 1964–1965 New York World's Fair, including "it's a small world" and attractions featuring the first human AA figures ever produced by Disney: Great Moments With Mr. Lincoln, Magic Skyway, and Carousel of Progress.

Over the years, various Disneyland attractions have come to life through Audio-Animatronics. In the summer of 2003, Lucky the Dinosaur, the first-ever free-roaming Audio-Animatronics creation, premiered at the Disneyland Resort. The startlingly lifelike creature—which can laugh, sneeze, bray, and even get the hiccups—was named one of the top inventions of 2003 by *Time* magazine and represents the next step forward in Audio-Animatronics technology—a technology originally "for the birds" that continues to captivate young and old alike.

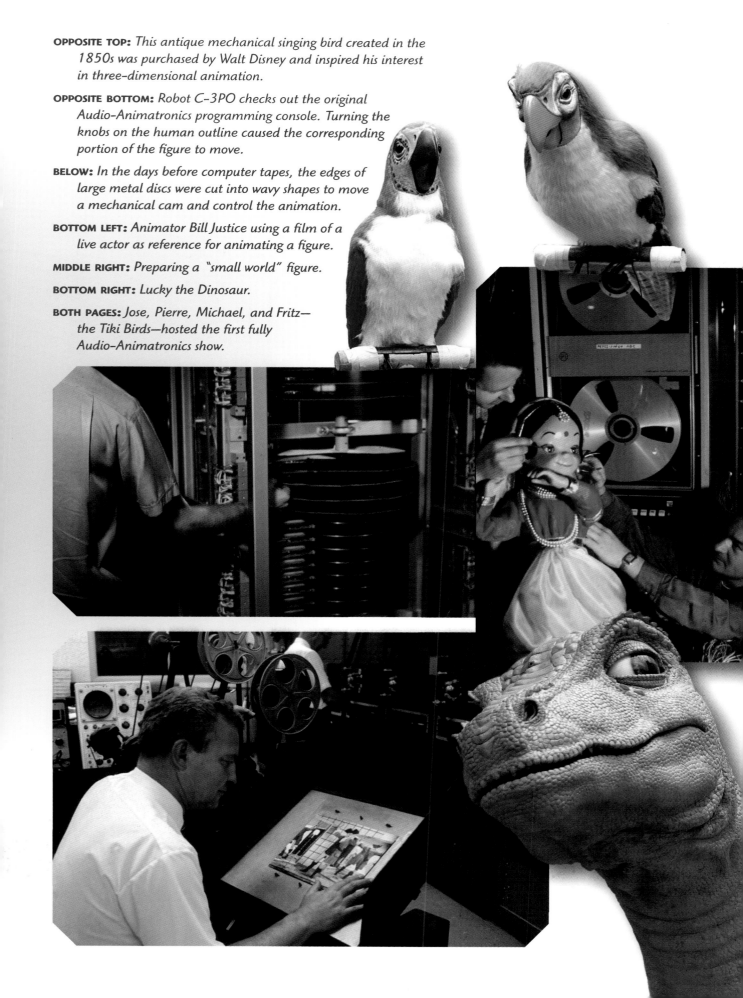

OPPOSITE TOP: *This antique mechanical singing bird created in the 1850s was purchased by Walt Disney and inspired his interest in three-dimensional animation.*

OPPOSITE BOTTOM: *Robot C–3PO checks out the original Audio-Animatronics programming console. Turning the knobs on the human outline caused the corresponding portion of the figure to move.*

BELOW: *In the days before computer tapes, the edges of large metal discs were cut into wavy shapes to move a mechanical cam and control the animation.*

BOTTOM LEFT: *Animator Bill Justice using a film of a live actor as reference for animating a figure.*

MIDDLE RIGHT: *Preparing a "small world" figure.*

BOTTOM RIGHT: *Lucky the Dinosaur.*

BOTH PAGES: *Jose, Pierre, Michael, and Fritz— the Tiki Birds—hosted the first fully Audio-Animatronics show.*

The Secrets of
AMERICA SINGS

America Sings, a salute to the great American songbook, opened on June 29, 1974, in the Carousel Theater in Tomorrowland. Hosted by Sam the Eagle, the attraction's theme song was naturally America's first popular song, "Yankee Doodle." The show literally traveled 'round through various eras, including Going South, Heading West, Gay Nineties, and Modern Times.

America Sings held more than a few secrets. In the Gay Nineties section "Golden Horseshoe" star Betty Taylor provided a rendition of her signature tune "Bill Bailey, Won't You Please Come Home" in the guise of a pink pig. In 1986, two geese from America Sings were reassigned as long-necked robots in the Star Tours queue.

When America Sings closed in 1988 many of its stars moved to Critter Country to comprise the supporting cast of Splash Mountain. (Now you know why they look so familiar!)

OPPOSITE: *Modern-day rockers spread "Joy to the World."*

CENTER: *A Gay Nineties waiter kicks up his pig knuckles.*

ABOVE: *The "Frontier Four" serenade with traditional Western favorites.*

RIGHT: *A son of the Old South.*

BELOW LEFT: *Saddle Sore Swanson croons the "Old Chisholm Trail."*

BELOW RIGHT: *The "Ta-Ra-Ra-Boom-De-Ay" finale of the Gay Nineties segment.*

The Carousel Theater opened on July 2, 1967, and was designed specifically to showcase the West Coast version of the Carousel of Progress attraction from the 1964–1965 New York World's Fair.

In 1974, the Carousel of Progress show moved to Walt Disney World, and in 1975 an all-new show, America Sings, took its place in the Carousel Theater as a nod to the upcoming American Bicentennial. The attraction starred 114 Audio-Animatronics performers who sang America's musical praises until the show closed in 1988.

The theater remained closed for a decade, when in 1998 a futuristic two-level interactive pavilion entitled Innoventions opened to showcase near-future high technology for the home, personal health, and leisure. The name "Tom Morrow," the robotic host of Innoventions, was once used as the director of flight operations for the Flight to the Moon attraction, and can be heard being paged in the Star Tours queue. The fondly remembered title tune from the Carousel of Progress, "There's a Great Big Beautiful Tomorrow," continues today as the theme song for Innoventions.

TOP LEFT: *"Father," the amiable and forward-looking host of the Carousel of Progress.*

TOP RIGHT: *Sam the Eagle and Ollie Owl (whose name was never used in the show) hosted America Sings.*

BOTTOM AND OPPOSITE BOTTOM: *Tomorrowland's robotic version of Tom Morrow welcomes guests to Innoventions.*

What was there before the Carousel Theater?

THIS PAGE: *In Disneyland, names can be deceiving. Take for example the case of The Space Bar. The name alone might conjure up visions of an intergalactic watering hole, filled with shady aliens and rocket jockeys. In actuality The Space Bar was a walk-up fast food restaurant located in prime Tomorrowland real estate to be later occupied by the Carousel Theater. The Space Bar served would-be space cadets delicious "Spaceburgers" and other appropriately named outer space fare. There were even examples of those futuristic modes of snacking convenience—vending machines! The future soon caught up with the Space Bar, however, and it closed to make way for the Carousel of Progress in September 1966.*

Secrets that hide beyond the Berm

PIRATES OF THE CARIBBEAN

"Ye come seekin' adventure and salty ol' pirates, eh?" Well, if you were looking for Pirates of the Caribbean prior to March 18, 1967, you would have been out of luck. Prior to the opening of the world-famous attraction, the site was home to Magnolia Park, a quiet, shady area between the Rivers of America and the Jungle Cruise. The centerpiece of Magnolia Park was an ornate bandstand that was originally situated in Town Square.

Initially planned as a basement walk-through attraction called "Pirate Wax Museum" (part of a larger complex called "Blue Bayou Mart"), construction began on the pirate project in 1961, thus forever erasing Magnolia Park. However, after an initial burst of construction, everything ceased so Walt could concentrate on the 1964–1965 New York World's Fair. For four years a giant hole remained in Disneyland.

With lessons learned from the Fair, Walt decided that the attraction, now dubbed Pirates of the Caribbean, would instead be an elaborate boat adventure featuring a cast of swashbuckling Audio-Animatronics buccaneers. Thus, all plans and construction began anew. As he would with The Haunted Mansion, Walt determined that most of the attraction would need to be housed "beyond the berm." Today, guests unknowingly descend into the original basement via a pair of waterfalls and ascend by, naturally, going up a waterfall!

MIDDLE AND BOTTOM: *During construction, the bandstand originally stood in Town Square. Before Opening Day, Walt had the bandstand moved to the Central Plaza (the current site of Plaza Gardens) so as not to obstruct views on Main Street, U.S.A. In 1956, the bandstand was moved yet again, this time to Magnolia Park in Adventureland. The bandstand stood there—on the future site of Pirates of the Caribbean—from 1956 to 1961.*

RIGHT: The Chicken Plantation restaurant was removed to make way for Pirates of the Caribbean. During construction, chicken dinners were served from a window in the construction fence (the white-roofed structure at top center, in the image below). But when Pirates opened, the chicken dinners had flown the coop for good.

ABOVE: When Pirates of the Caribbean was still being planned as a walk-through, construction actually began in 1961. The steel seen here was later removed for New Orleans Square. Note the absence of any construction "beyond the berm."

Secrets that hide beyond the Berm
THE HAUNTED MANSION

ABOVE: *The Haunted Mansion "home" and "show building" under construction in 1963. To the right center of the photo can be seen the water tower and depot of the Frontierland Train Station. Notice how the tracks of the Disneyland Railroad cut right through the center of the attraction.*

LEFT: *A billboard announces the long-awaited opening of The Haunted Mansion in 1969.*

BELOW: *The Southern plantation–inspired home of The Haunted Mansion begins to take shape in 1963. When completed, the house remained vacant for six years.*

The concept of creating a New Orleans Square, featuring a "Haunted House," had been under consideration by Walt Disney dating back to 1958. In 1963 construction began on the antebellum Southern manor (near the site of the Chicken Plantation restaurant) that would officially become the riverfront home of The Haunted Mansion. However, the house would actually remain vacant along the Rivers of America until the attraction officially opened on August 29, 1969.

In planning The Haunted Mansion, Walt and his Imagineers realized that a large "show" building was needed to house a majority of the attraction's elaborate sets. In order to make best use of the limited real estate that the Mansion occupied it was decided to extend the attraction "beyond the berm."

Today, as Haunted Mansion guests descend in the Stretching Room and walk the length of the Portrait Corridor, they are actually (and seamlessly) walking under the tracks of the Disneyland Railroad and into the backstage area of Disneyland. Guests return to the world of the living by ascending a moving walkway, passing the spirit of "Little Leota" who beckons them to "Hurry back! Hurry Back! Be sure to bring your death certificate."

What was there before
Pirates of the Caribbean and The Haunted Mansion?

HOLIDAYLAND

Often referred to as the "lost" land of Disneyland, Holidayland did indeed exist. Morphing in early plans from a salute to rural America behind Main Street and Tomorrowland to a "Recreation Park," the area formally premiered as "Holidayland" on June 16, 1957.

Located roughly where New Orleans Square and The Haunted Mansion stand today, Holidayland was capable of accommodating over 7,000 guests, and was designed as the ideal locale for group events, including company picnics, family reunions, or any large social function.

Holidayland featured its own admission gate, a baseball diamond, and accommodations for volleyball, horseshoes, shuffleboard, square dancing, and other outdoor activities.

The landmark of Holidayland was its gigantic red and white candy-striped tent, featuring a stage (where the Mouseketeers would occasionally perform) and rows and rows of picnic tables. Holidayland was plagued by a lack of shade, nighttime lighting (the area was not open in the evenings), and restrooms, plus utilization issues (the groups who used it were only available on weekends). These problems, plus its isolation from Disneyland itself all led to the demise of Holidayland, which closed in 1961.

TOP: *The Entrance to Holidayland, located just west of where the Indiana Jones™ attraction stands today.*

ABOVE: *A featured part of Holidayland was a children's play area, with equipment themed to a land in the Park—here, Sleeping Beauty Castle in Fantasyland.*

TOP: *Holidayland extended from the western border of Frontierland to West Street (now Disneyland Drive).*

ABOVE LEFT: *A standard playground, themed to Frontierland but not very Disney-like, inside Holidayland.*

ABOVE RIGHT: *An admission ticket to Holidayland eventually included admission to Disneyland, but even that could not save the ill-fated "land."*

AN OLD FASHIONED PICNIC

in HOLIDAYLAND at DISNEYLAND

GOOD ONLY SAT., JULY 2, 1960

ADMIT ONE CHILD

Good for admission to Disneyland through Special Gate in Holidayland, or may be presented at Holidayland Ticket Windows for full credit toward purchase of a Ticket Book which INCLUDES Disneyland admission.

Established price $ .60

15¢ ADMIT ONE 15¢ CHILD to HOLIDAYLAND

Secrets That Hid Beyond the Berm
TOONTOWN

According to Disney legend, Mickey Mouse founded Toontown back in the 1930s as a secret getaway for him and his animated pals whenever they needed a break from the glitz and glamour of Hollywood. Walt Disney was the only non-Toon who knew of its existence. Mickey's Toontown remained a highly guarded secret "beyond the berm" of Disneyland until Mickey decided to throw open its gates to an eager public in 1993.

Prior to the creation of Mickey's Toontown, the three-acre area that is now the site of such fun-filled attractions as Roger Rabbit's Car Toon Spin, Gadget's Go-Coaster, Jolly Trolley, and the homes of Mickey, Minnie, Donald, and Goofy was off-limits to "Toons" and Disneyland guests alike. Truly "backstage," the site was separated from Disneyland by Winston Road, a public roadway literally on the other side of the railroad tracks from the park. The area was used as the launching site of the "Fantasy in the Sky" fireworks, a small nursery, and a storage area for various large attraction props and parade vehicles.

Today, the Circle D Corral, the backstage home of Disneyland's award-winning stable of horses, remains directly adjacent to Mickey's Toontown, and features several structures original to the property back in the 1950s.

BELOW CLOCKWISE: *Three Toontown favorites—Roger Rabbit's Car Toon Spin, Chip 'n' Dale's Treehouse, and Goofy's Bounce House.*

ABOVE: *Prior to the addition of Mickey's Toontown, a city street called Winston Road (seen at left edge of photo) separated the park from its "backstage" area. Some of the buildings in the upper portion of the photo, which are part of the Circle D Corral, are original to the ranches seen on page 16 and still stand today. Keen eyes will notice the 24-foot Christmas star which would adorn the top of the Matterhorn from 1961 until the mid-1970s.*

The Secret of THE CASEY JR. ROLLER COASTER

Based on the determined little train featured in Walt Disney's animated feature *Dumbo*, the seemingly benign Casey Jr. Circus Train that today huffs and puffs in Fantasyland began its life not as a charming and delightful railroad journey through Storybook Land but as a rollicking and thrilling roller coaster—the first one ever designated for Disneyland.

Initial plans called for the little train to race through the barren hills of Fantasyland. However, after test runs were conducted, concerns were raised about its effectiveness as a roller coaster and the accompanying maintenance issues that would be involved, so Casey Jr. quickly lost its status as Disneyland's first thrill ride. Nonetheless, the Casey Jr. Circus Train did appear as an attraction on Opening Day but was then immediately shuttered for fine tuning. Casey Jr. returned to service on July 31, 1955, and has been performing to perfection ever since.

Today the Casey Jr. Circus Train, which is narrated by Dumbo's good friend Timothy Q. Mouse, remains a fun-filled trip through Storybook Land, whose miniature houses were added in 1956. The look of the train is a loving tribute to the whimsical design of its namesake from the film, with ornate detail and benches that were originally a part of the 1875 merry-go-round that was eventually transformed into King Arthur Carrousel.

BACKGROUND AND BELOW: *Disney artist Bruce Bushman's original concept sketches for Casey Jr. Circus Train.*

OPPOSITE TOP: *The Casey Jr. Circus Train traverses a trestle in Fantasyland. The eucalyptus trees in the background are native to Disneyland (though not Anaheim). They were used as wind-breaks in the orange groves that were present before the Park was built.*

OPPOSITE MIDDLE AND BOTTOM: *The Casey Jr. Circus Train goes for test runs in 1955 on a mock-up track.*

Secrets of
UnBuilt Attractions

Walt Disney once said "Disneyland will never be completed as long as there is imagination left in the world." That maxim continues today with an ever-evolving landscape of new adventures, shows, and attractions. However, through the years, secrets regarding projects "of the future" leaked out of the secret labs of WED Enterprises (now known as Walt Disney Imagineering), or Walt himself would provide sneak previews of new additions to Disneyland on TV or in print.

Some of the concepts found their way into other Disney theme parks, or had elements lifted and incorporated into alternate attractions. Many were developed and discarded. Nonetheless, the Disneyland attractions and "lands" that might have been, and never were, have become legendary and continue to fascinate Disney fans, begging the question, "What if . . . ?"

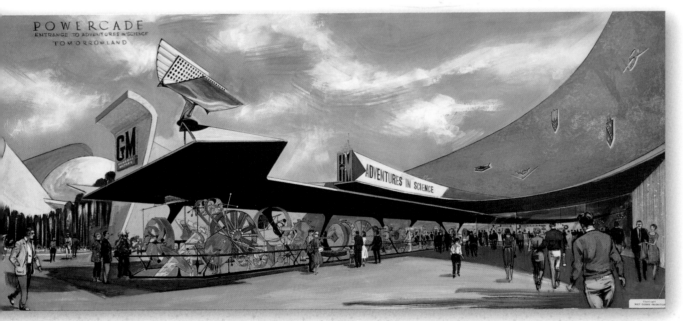

TOP: *Proposed for 1960 was a "duck bump" attraction themed around Donald Duck, a Disney water version of the classic amusement park bumper cars.*

ABOVE: *Highlighted on the Disneyland souvenir map of 1958 was a "future attraction" entitled "Adventures in Science," a history-of-science exhibit proposed for the site now occupied by Space Mountain.*

ABOVE: *A "Chinatown" adjunct to Main Street was proposed in 1959, featuring an elaborate dinner show hosted by Confucius, who would have been the first human Audio-Animatronics figure.*

LEFT: *An early concept for Frontierland had guests riding mechanical horses in front of a movie screen, putting them in the middle of the action.*

BELOW: *Rock Candy Mountain was originally planned for Fantasyland until the model, made of real candy, began to melt and was pecked to pieces by the local birds —and by the modelmakers!*

More Secrets of
UnBuilt Attractions

From 1973 to 1989 Main Street, U.S.A. featured an attraction called Disneyland Presents a Preview of Coming Attractions. During those 16 years, numerous young, aspiring Disney Imagineers and Disneyland fans marveled at a series of intricate models and concept renderings detailing future additions to Disneyland. Some of the "previews" actually became a reality such as Big Thunder Mountain Railroad and Space Mountain. Two of the most intriguing "previews" showcased a mysterious Discovery Bay and a colorful and light-hearted Dumbo's Circusland.

Discovery Bay, planned as a transition point between Frontierland and Fantasyland, was loosely themed around a San Francisco, Barbary Coast seaside port filled with attractions inspired by the age of discovery and the visions of Jules Verne. Dumbo's Circusland, inspired by Walt Disney's 1941 classic animated film *Dumbo*, was envisioned as a major part of a renovated Fantasyland, with both the Casey Jr. Circus Train and Dumbo the Flying Elephant relocated to this new area.

Dumbo's Circusland never became a reality, but elements of Discovery Bay were incorporated into Discoveryland at Disneyland Resort Paris in France.

OPPOSITE PAGE, TOP TO BOTTOM: *The proposed Discovery Bay's attractions included a Gallery of Illusions, a Voyage Thru Time boat ride with near-disastrous consequences, and the elaborate—and thrilling—Spark Cap Electric Loop Coaster.*

ABOVE: *A high-flying "hot-air" balloon ascent attraction would have connected Discovery Bay and Dumbo's Circusland.*

BELOW: *Two elaborate "dark rides" were developed for Dumbo's Circusland: the nuttiness of Dumbo's Circus and Mickey's Madhouse.*

INTERNATIONAL STREET

In 1956 Disneyland guests encountered a sign in Town Square announcing the soon-to-open "International Street." Curious guests could peek through holes in the construction wall to view "progress" on this exciting new area of the park. When guests looked through the holes they viewed a 3-D picture of the model of International Street, thus providing guests with a unique, behind-the-scenes glimpse of things to come . . . sort of. The construction wall guests peered through simply hid the "backstage" area of Main Street, no building or construction of International Street ever occurred.

International Street was originally conceived as "International Land," to be built just north of Tomorrowland. Both the street and the land would have highlighted the architectural styles and cultures of many nations around the world. As guests walked along the streets, no matter which way they turned, they would encounter a different architectural influence, featuring the iconic imagery of Europe, Asia, and the Americas.

The projects never became a reality at Disneyland, but the concept did serve as inspiration for World Showcase in *Epcot* at the Walt Disney World Resort in Florida.

THIS PAGE: *Never-before-seen close-up photographs of the model created in 1956 for International Street. Though the Imagineers usually create dozens of concept sketches for their new attractions, not a single illustration was ever created for International Street. This model has been carefully preserved, and stands as the only record of the concept.*

BELOW: *Conceptual layout for International Land, to be located just beyond Tomorrowland.*

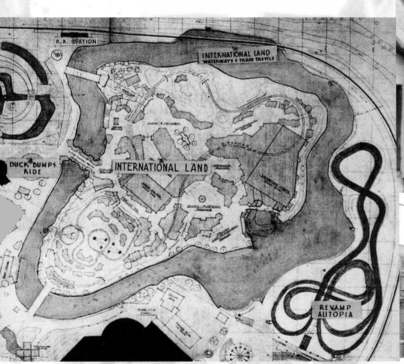

LIBERTY STREET

LIBERTY STREET and LIBERTY SQUARE.

OPPOSITE SHORE IN REDUCED SCALE

WATER FRONT SCENE AT END OF LIBERTY S

SHOPS AND EXHIBITS

LIBERTY STREET

LIBERTY SQUARE

EXHIBIT

TAVERN

SHIP CHANDLER

VIEW OF AARBOR & DOCKS
WITH SHIPS AT ANCHOR (IN BACKING)

ABOVE: *Guests would begin their stroll down Liberty Street encountering authentic shops showcasing the trades and artisans of the era, including candle makers, blacksmiths, glassblowers, printers, and furniture makers. In the distance, guests could see a realistic waterfront scene featuring majestic sailing ships anchored in a bay. Turning right into Liberty Square, guests would encounter a reproduction of Independence Hall, featuring The Hall of Presidents, the signature attraction of Liberty Street.*

Next on the Disneyland roster of things to come, replacing International Street, was the concept of "Liberty Street." Planned as a salute to America's Revolutionary War–era founding, the new area would replicate the look and feel of colonial America of the late 1700s, featuring architecture representing all 13 original American colonies.

The main attraction on Liberty Street was to be The Hall of Presidents, showcased inside Independence Hall and featuring a show called One Nation Under God, an elaborate theater presentation focusing on the fundamental principles that have guided American history. The show was also to feature an impressive roster of Audio-Animatronics figures of every President of the United States—from Washington to Eisenhower.

Although Liberty Street and The Hall of Presidents were never produced for Disneyland, their concepts and show elements directly influenced the 1964 creation of one of Walt Disney's most

ABOVE: *In 1958 the venerable Town Square sign that had once announced the grand opening of "International Street" was converted to announcing an all-new addition to Disneyland— "Liberty Street."*

personal and successful attractions, Great Moments With Mr. Lincoln. Liberty Street (re-dubbed Liberty Square) was eventually created in 1971 as part of Magic Kingdom Park at Walt Disney World—complete with The Hall of Presidents, which used many of the actual audio recordings created in 1958 under Walt Disney's supervision.

ABOVE: *Liberty Street would have been home to all the Presidents, including Mr. Lincoln, seen in this concept sketch by Disney artist Sam McKim.*

EDISON SQUARE

Planned to open in springtime 1959 near the Plaza Hub was an all-new Disneyland addition called "Edison Square." This ambitious concept was designed to be a bit more urban in execution and feel than the Midwest-inspired Main Street. Set circa 1918, the charming square would represent the budding age of electricity and would prominently feature a statue of its namesake, Thomas A. Edison, at its center.

The main attraction of Edison Square would be a show called Harnessing the Lightning, a four-act history of electricity as seen through the eyes of four generations of a typical American family as they experience the wondrous advances in electrical technology.

Like its predecessors, International Street and Liberty Street, Edison Square never became a Disneyland reality. However, the Harnessing the Lightning attraction and other elements of Edison Square were not forgotten and were incorporated into one of the most fondly remembered Disneyland attractions of all time—the Carousel of Progress.

DARK T&G WAINSCOTING

WALLPAPER ABOVE

GLASS FOR PRIVACY

EXPOSED PLUMBING—
"NEW-FANGLED" SHOWER OVER TUB WITH CIRCULAR CURTAIN-RING — PERHAPS WATER CAN "GURGLE-SPURT" ON TIMED CYCLE FROM VARIOUS FIXTURES —

LINOLEUM

TOILET TANK TO EMPTY (TIMED CYCLE) — NOISY FLUSH (TO CONTRAST WITH MODERN BATHROOM)

WHITE MARBLE LAVATORY TOP — EXPOSED PIPES

• OLD BATH-ROOM •

IF PLUMBING- HOT WATER HEATER

WOOD BOX & COAL SCUTTLE

OIL LAMPS ON STORAGE SHELF

WATER PUMP ?

ETC ANTIQUATED PLUMBING

HOME-CANNING — PUTTING UP CHERRIES - PEARS, ETC LADLE-PANS MASON JARS ETC

OPPOSITE: *Concept sketch of Edison Square by Disney artist Sam McKim.*

TOP AND RIGHT: *An old bathroom and an antiquated kitchen were showcased by artist Sam McKim in Harnessing the Lightning, the show that inspired the Carousel of Progress.*

BELOW: *Rather than riding in a revolving theater, guests would walk past decade-by-decade vignettes showing how life has been made easier by the introduction of electricity, as seen in this sketch by Disney Legend John Hench.*

The "icing" on the Disneyland cake

ENCHANTMENT

The word "enchantment" can be defined in many ways. At Disneyland, however, enchantment is easily defined by the faces of young and old alike that "meet and greet" with the beloved Disney characters. The appeal and allure of the Disney characters is irresistible and it is a strong-willed individual, child or adult, who can resist the natural inclination to react with a smile to the antics of Mickey, Minnie, Donald, Pluto, Goofy, and all their friends. It has become almost an international tradition to get your picture taken or receive an autograph from one of the Disney Characters at Disneyland. Through the years the Disney Characters have welcomed children of all ages, from all backgrounds and conditions. And all it takes to believe in magic is to watch the elation that comes upon a small child's face as he or she intuitively communicates with Mickey Mouse in person.

The Enchantment of
THE EARLY DAYS

Since the Opening Day parade in July 1955, Mickey Mouse and his pals have been the official hosts of "The Happiest Place on Earth." In those early days, the characters were traditionally found in front of the Main Street Train Station and the "Flower Mickey" planter, or just inside Town Square. As the park grew, it was not unusual to find Peter Pan, Captain Hook, and Mr. Smee frolicking around Skull Rock, Brer Bear and Brer Fox chasing Brer Rabbit through New Orleans Square, or Snow White and all Seven Dwarfs marching through Fantasyland.

Over the years, like all of us, the Disney Characters have changed and evolved in appearance. However, their innate charm has remained true. Today, as in the past, the Disney Characters remain among the most photographed celebrities in the world.

TOP: *Mickey and Minnie meet friends on Main Street in the late 1950s.*

ABOVE AND OPPOSITE LEFT: *The Seven Dwarfs assemble for a group photo.*

LEFT: *Alice in Wonderland, the White Rabbit, and the Mad Hatter say "hello" from Fantasyland in the mid–1960s.*

ABOVE: *Three "Little" Pigs?*

BELOW: *An unusual gathering of Mickey, Minnie, Chip 'n' Dale, Thumper, and Alice in Wonderland, in the early 1970s.*

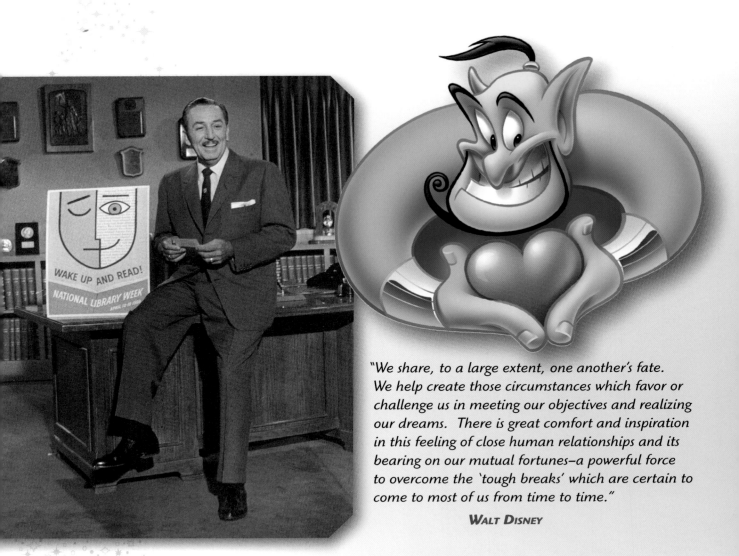

"We share, to a large extent, one another's fate. We help create those circumstances which favor or challenge us in meeting our objectives and realizing our dreams. There is great comfort and inspiration in this feeling of close human relationships and its bearing on our mutual fortunes—a powerful force to overcome the 'tough breaks' which are certain to come to most of us from time to time."

WALT DISNEY

The Enchantment of CARING

Each year, Disney makes dreams come true through partnerships with wish-granting organizations such as the Make-A-Wish Foundation®. The Make-A-Wish Foundation, the largest wish-granting partner of DisneyHand, grants the wishes of children with life-threatening medical conditions to enrich the human experience with hope, strength, and joy. The number one wish of all children they serve is a trip to a Disney park. In 2005, Disney will celebrate 50 Years of Wishes by helping make the 50,000 Disney theme park wish come true with the Make-A-Wish Foundation, exactly 25 years after we helped fulfilled the wish of the very first Make-A-Wish® child . . . a trip to Disneyland.

For more information on DisneyHand's outreach projects and programs around the world, please visit us at www.DisneyHand.com.

RIGHT TOP AND BOTTOM: *Since 1948, when Walt and his animators designed the Toys for Tots train logo still in use today, to the present day as Disney characters deliver gifts and cheer to children in hospitals around the world, we have believed in making the dreams of children and families come true.*

BELOW AND OPPOSITE BOTTOM: *Caring—then, now, and forever.*

THESE PAGES: *Enchantment at work at Disneyland, powered by smiles and a touch of pixie dust.*

FOREVER DREAMING

Walt's dream will never be complete

It was Walt Disney's desire that Disneyland continue to grow and evolve. In February 2001, Walt's original dream of Disneyland was joined by its sister park, Disney's California Adventure—an all-new Disney theme park experience, where Disney magic meets California fun. Disney's California Adventure covers 55 acres and celebrates the lifestyle, regions, and allure of the Golden State. Designed with a high energy, slightly irreverent "pop culture" attitude, the park features a variety of themed areas—including Hollywood Pictures Backlot, Golden State, a bug's land, Condor Flats, and Paradise Pier.

Forever Dreaming of MAGIC

Since opening on February 8, 2001, Disney's California Adventure has grown to include some of the most advanced, innovative, and entertaining shows and attractions presented at the Disneyland Resort, including Soarin' Over California, *The Twilight Zone Tower of Terror™*, a bug's land, and Playhouse Disney—Live on Stage. Popular annual special events such as Fiesta Latina, ABC Super Soap Weekend, and ABC Prime Time Weekend provide guests with the chance to meet some of their favorite TV and music stars.

Once guests pass under the "Golden State Bridge" and through Sunshine Plaza, they enter a three-dimensional, fanciful postcard representation of the sights and sounds of California. From the beach culture of Paradise Pier to the glitz and glamour of Hollywood Pictures Backlot to the romance and adventure of Golden State, guests experience an amalgam of California culture and fun.

ABOVE: *The impressive gates of the Hollywood Pictures Backlot were inspired by the sets of the classic films of Hollywood's early silent movies.*

ABOVE: *The Disney Animation attraction presents an impressive and elaborate overview and hands-on experience showcasing the wonders of Disney's rich animation legacy.*

BELOW LEFT: *Flik is your host in the signature attraction of a bug's land— It's Tough to be a Bug!, a fun-filled 3-D film experience.*

BELOW RIGHT: *Hopper, the villain from the Disney/Pixar film A Bug's Life comes to life via amazing Audio-Animatronics technology in It's Tough to be a Bug!*

Forever Dreaming of
CHALLENGES

Guests to Disney's California Adventure can find myriad adventures and attractions that simultaneously thrill, amaze, and challenge the imagination. In this microcosm of the "Golden State" guests can explore its great outdoors from up in the sky to down on the ground—stretching from the high deserts of Southern California to the rushing rivers of the northern "Gold Rush" region.

In a salute to the state's extraordinary aviation history, guests can literally glide through the skies over California, while those less inclined to leave Mother Earth can hike the paths of the state's great forests along the Redwood Creek Challenge Trail. But on a hot day there is no better place to be than shooting the ice-cold rapids around Grizzly Peak on the Grizzly River Run.

THIS PAGE: *The flagship attraction of Disney's California Adventure is Soarin' Over California, an exhilarating flight over the scenic wonders of the Golden State.*

LEFT AND BELOW: *The Grizzly River Run provides guests with a thrilling (and occasionally chilling) white-water adventure through the redwoods and around the base of Grizzly Peak.*

BOTTOM: *The Redwood Creek Challenge Trail re-creates the world of California's park rangers in a high-energy obstacle course.*

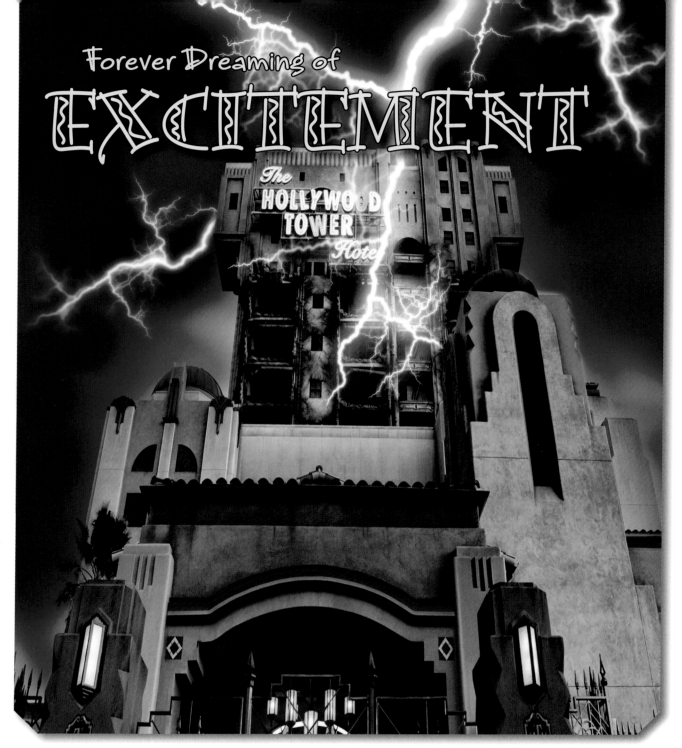

Forever Dreaming of
EXCITEMENT

The Twilight Zone Tower of Terror™, an unforgettable supernatural adventure in the Hollywood Pictures Backlot, features a breathtaking "faster-than-the-speed of gravity" climactic free fall from the 13th floor of the Hollywood Tower Hotel. Based on a "lost episode" of the classic *Twilight Zone* television series, the attraction looms 183 feet (the tallest attraction at the Disneyland Resort) and tempts guests to leave reality—and their stomachs—behind. The crumbly yet still stately landmark exhibits an air of foreboding, especially to sharp-eyed guests who may notice that part of the building seems to have been struck by an oddly violent bolt of lightning, exposing the elevator shafts and revealing a glimpse of the "terror" inside.

BELOW: *The Maliboomer, Orange Stinger, and Golden Zephyr provide Chip 'n' Dale and friends with a fun-filled backdrop at Paradise Pier.*

RIGHT: *The mascot of Dinosaur Jack's Sunglass Shack and one of the zeppelin-shaped stainless steel spaceships of the Golden Zephyr.*

BOTTOM: *All it takes is 4.7 seconds to launch guests from 0 to 55 mph on an amazing ride on the California Screamin' roller coaster in Paradise Pier.*

INDEX

"Disneyland will always be building and growing and adding new things . . . new ways of having fun, of learning things, and sharing the many exciting adventures which may be experienced here in the company of family and friends."

Walt Disney

Disne...

Fantasyland

ADVENTURELAND